Memorable Meals

FIRST EDITION
Copyright © Nancy Wood Moorman

Printed in Hong Kong
By Eakin Press
An Imprint of Sunbelt Media, Inc.
P.O. Drawer 990159 ★ Austin, Texas

2 3 4 5 6 7 8 9

ISBN 1-57168-210-4

Credits:
Bill DeBold, photography; Rose Rankin, food styling; Venetia DeBose, design and typography

Memorable Meals

A DELICIOUS BLEND OF CLASSIC AND CONTEMPORARY CUISINES

by Nancy Wood Moorman

*This book is dedicated to
my daughter, Ramona Wood Moorman,
and my sister, Kathryn Wood Johnston.*

*Their untimely deaths taught me
the value of treasuring every moment.*

Contents

PREFACE

When I began teaching cooking classes in 1977, French was considered the only *haute cuisine*. As a result, I felt the need to master French techniques and pass them along to my students. I still maintain that some knowledge of French technique is an excellent basis from which to become a creative cook. Understanding the potential of eggs, yeast, pastry, sauces, frying and sautéeing instills considerable self-confidence. Rather than teach technique classes, however, I utilize menu classes. I find that students seem to absorb the basic techniques with less effort when preparing an actual meal.

Over the years, my classes have evolved to cater to more sophisticated tastes as well as the growing interest in cuisines from around the world. Food processors and the ready availa-bility of once rare fresh herbs and exotic ingredients have simplified cooking and made it possible for home cooks to master and enjoy an almost limitless choice of cuisines.

For this book, I have selected a wide variety of recipes I think you will enjoy. Some reflect my French training. Some are family or personal favorites, but all are ones that have been used with great success by me and my students for entertaining. Many have been inspired by my former teachers, famous chefs or food I have enjoyed in wonderful restaurants. My hope is that they will inspire and excite you as they have me and that you will use this book as a springboard to create your own variations and have great fun in the kitchen.

The recipes have been tested and improved upon by my students, to whom I give much credit. Even those that sound difficult or seem time consuming are actually quite simple and can usually be prepared in stages or well in advance, making them ideal for entertaining. I hope you will try them. They work and they are good; however, to experience the real joy and creativity to be derived from cooking, I encourage you to use them only as a guide.

Don't worry too much about measurements or oven temperatures. Until writing this book, I did not own a measuring spoon. Except when making pastry or certain egg dishes, measurements can be relatively flexible. Feel free to change and adapt recipes to suit your individual taste and create your own "signature dish." What's important is to relax, express yourself, and, above all, have fun. Remember, "cooking light" means more than just leaving out the cream or abandoning the butter.

Because entertaining at home is uncommon these days, most people consider an invitation to your home a special treat. I believe that entertaining at home is doubly fun for the hostess as it provides an opportunity to create something unique and special along with the added pleasure of sharing it with those you care about. Whether it's a casual backyard cookout or a formal celebration dinner, it can be made memorable with just a few creative touches and a little extra effort. To foster your creativity, I have included menu and wine suggestions. Again, these are meant to serve as a springboard for your own wonderful ideas.

Cooking, as you may have guessed, is my passion. It is a source of creative expression. It is a constant delight and challenge. It is a source of comfort and refuge. It is excellent therapy. But most of all, it is a joy that is enhanced many times over when shared with family and friends. So, don your aprons, plug in your processors, and see how many wonderful ways you can make these recipes *your* very own. I promise your family and friends will enjoy and treasure your memorable meals.

ACKNOWLEDGEMENTS

I would like to especially thank the following people for their invaluable contributions to this book:

PAT ROSS, of Jackson, Mississippi, my first teacher. Her enthusiasm and relaxed manner truly inspired me. I try to emulate her teaching style to this day.

BETTY MOORMAN, my mother-in-law, for allowing me access to her black and white mottled recipe box. It still produces some of the best menus in South Texas.

SALLY HELLAND, my assistant and dear friend. She has been by my side for every teaching session for 15 years. When she quits, I do.

MARY DENNY, my editor. Without her knowledge and encouragement, I would never have written this book.

EMILY CANAVAN, who took over the typing when I was at the end of my rope.

MANNY LUNA AND E. B. CASTRO of The Rose Shop. Their advice and help with the flowers used in the photography sessions once again helped make an important event in my life special.

ALAN DREEBEN, FERNANDO DE LUNA, AND MARK MATTINGLY of Block Distributing. They spent many hours helping me match wines with food.

Most importantly, I thank my students. I have learned more about food from them than from any teacher or class I have attended. Because of their enthusiasm, I was able to develop a career that helped me through some incredibly rocky times. I owe them my deepest gratitude.

Finally, I thank my husband, JEFF, for not destroying my purple notebook of recipes, and my son, LEW, for helping me simplify my writing. Their patience and support while I worked non-stop for many months on this project is greatly appreciated.

Before You Begin

These notes about ingredients and techniques may come in helpful. Almost every recipe in the book requires one or more of the pieces of equipment listed.

—INGREDIENTS—

BUTTER: In all recipes, I use unsalted butter. *Margarine is not an option.*

EGGS: When eggs are called for, use large eggs.

FLOUR: Unless a specific flour is called for, use unbleached white. All purpose white may be used, but most serious cooks prefer the unbleached white.

CHOCOLATE: For home cooks, Baker's, Hershey's, or Nestle's is fine. When I use white chocolate, I use Lindt or Tobler. Always melt chocolate in a double boiler.

GARLIC: The size of garlic cloves varies greatly. I suggest using the largest cloves possible. Do not substitute elephant garlic. It is a different herb altogether.

HERBS: Use fresh herbs whenever possible, unless a recipe specifically calls for dried. (Many herbs, such as basil, taste entirely different when dried. Fresh and dried rosemary, however, are quite similar.) You must use twice the amount of fresh herbs to achieve the same intensity of flavor as a dried herb. Most herbs are easy to grow in pots or a small garden and make beautiful decorations for platters as well as flavorful additions to food.

STOCK VS. BROTH: Stock is a term I use to describe a broth that is homemade. It happens naturally when you cook a chicken in seasoned water. For beef stock, it is necessary to brown beef bones with celery, onion, carrot, bay leaf, thyme, oregano, marjoram, salt, and pepper. Brown in 350° degree oven, about an hour or until very brown. Deglaze pan with water or any type of alcohol. Cover with water and simmer 3 to 4 hours, adding additional water as necessary. In the interest of time and convenience however, I have recommended a good canned broth whenever possible. To differentiate, I refer to the homemade version as *stock* and the canned variety as *broth*.

PEPPER: Every chef I know recommends only freshly cracked black pepper. It is by far the best choice. But I must admit I often use canned black pepper—a sin in cooking circles—but it is certainly permissible for the home cook.

BOVRIL OR DEMI-GLACE: Bovril is a natural beef extract that I frequently use to enrich gravies. Demi-glace Gold and Glace de Poulet Gold are beef and chicken concentrates used in sauces. Forgotten Tradition is another excellent brand of demi-glace. These may be found at gourmet grocery stores or specialty cooking stores such as Williams-Sonoma. Another perfectly acceptable brand, Better than Bouillon, is usually available at local supermarkets.

BREAD CRUMBS: Some of my recipes call for untoasted, fresh bread crumbs. These are easy to make by putting the bread of choice in a food processor and processing until crumbs form. Crumbs can be frozen, so make more than you need. Canned bread crumbs cannot be substituted for fresh ones.

VENISON: This low fat game meat is becoming increasingly available to the home cook. Venison racks can be purchased from Good Heart, 6614 Seidel #30, San Antonio, Texas 78209. Or call toll free 1-888-466-3992 to order.

— T E C H N I Q U E S —

BAIN MARIE: This baking method is generally used for dishes that are baked with eggs, such as flans, mousses, and timbales. It involves placing the baking dish or dishes into a larger pan filled with boiling water. Ideally the water's depth should be 2/3 of the height of the molds or pans being baked. The important thing is to use enough water so it will not evaporate during baking. Usually an inch of water is sufficient.

DEGLAZING: Meat or poultry that has been sautéed leaves flavorful brown bits clinging to the bottom of the pan. Remove the sautéed meat, add some type of liquid or alcohol, such as wine, brandy, Marsala, etc., and over medium heat, scrape up the brown bits with a spatula. Add remaining ingredients as specified for the sauce or gravy. Our grandmothers made cream gravy by deglazing the meat pan with water.

BREADING: To get a wonderful crust on fried or sautéed meats or vegetables, dip them first in flour seasoned with salt and pepper, then in lightly beaten egg, and finally in fresh bread crumbs, cracker meal, or coating of choice. The flour and egg steps never change.

EGG GLAZE: An egg wash is made by mixing one raw egg with one tablespoon of water. It is brushed over pastry or bread before baking to help it brown. It is also used to glue decorative shapes of dough to bread or pastry.

ROUX: A roux is made of equal parts fat and flour and used to thicken a sauce or soup. The basic formula I use is 4 tablespoons butter (or other fat) and 4 tablespoons flour will thicken 3-4 cups of liquid. Melt butter in sauté pan, add flour , and stir 1-2 minutes, or until no traces of flour remain. Add 2 cups liquid all at once. Turn heat to high and whisk until mixture is thick. If mixture becomes too thick, which is probable–and a nice turn of events–thin it down with additional liquid until desired consistency is reached.

SEASONING WITH SALT AND PEPPER: I rarely give specific amounts of salt and pepper. Taste, taste and taste again. Let this be your guide. Good cooks are not afraid to season generously. Usually, if a dish falls a little flat, it needs more salt.

REDUCING CREAM: When a recipe calls for reducing cream, it's best to do it in a wide-bottomed pan. Use high heat and do not worry; it will not burn. Cream that has been reduced in half will turn a vanilla color. If cream does begin to boil over, whisk it with a balloon whisk to remove some of the air and bring cream back down.

REFRESHING: This technique involves plunging hot food into ice cold water in order to stop the cooking process. It also seals color into green vegetables so they may be prepared well before serving and still retain their color. Today many chefs prefer not to use this technique because they believe it washes out nutrients and flavor. However, when cooking for a large crowd, it is nice to have this technique available.

ROASTING PEPPERS: Wash peppers. Preheat broiler. Place peppers on pan under broiler until charred on all sides. The first side may take 10-15 minutes. Turn peppers. The second side will take considerably less time. Place in paper bag or bowl covered with plastic wrap until cool enough to handle. Peel and seed peppers. Use immediately or freeze in plastic freezer bags until needed.

BASIC PASTRY DOUGH: Pastry dough may be made with butter or Crisco or a combination. Crisco makes pastry flaky, butter adds taste. There are several variations of pastry dough in this book and they are particularly suited to the specific recipe. The one I have committed to memory and that is my all purpose personal favorite is this: 1 1/4 cups flour, dash of salt, 8 tablespoons butter, cut into tablespoons, 1/3 cup cold water. Put flour, butter, and salt in food processor and process until mixture resembles little peas. With machine on, add water. Process only until dough begins to form a ball. Remove dough from processor and form into a ball. Dough should be usable immediately.

— E Q U I P M E N T —

FOOD PROCESSOR: This wonderful machine has changed the life of the home cook. I consider it a "must have." Unless I am grating or slicing, I always use the steel blade.

MINI-FOOD PROCESSOR: This is a great asset and, in my opinion, another "must have." It is handy for making citrus zest, mincing garlic or parsley, and the perfect size for one recipe of vinaigrette. You'll use it every day!

BLENDER: I consider the blender an essential piece of equipment. It is excellent for puréeing soups and making salsas for many southwestern dishes.

HAND-HELD MIXER: Another necessity for whipping cream, egg whites, or potatoes.

GRILL PAN: This is a heavy cast iron skillet with a ridged bottom. I use mine frequently for making attractive grill marks on meat, fish, or vegetables.

FEEMSTER: This is a small inexpensive hand-held slicer that makes quick work of slicing vegetables. Newer vegetable slicers are on the market but this is a great stand-by.

PLASTIC SQUEEZE BOTTLES: When filled with sauces, vinaigrettes, or flavored oils, these are great tools for decorating dishes. Buy lots!

PASTRY CLOTH/ROLLING PIN: A heavy-duty pastry cloth makes rolling pastry a breeze and the work area easy to clean up. I recommend a heavy-duty rolling pin without handles.

MOLDS: Many recipes call for 6-ounce ramekins, soufflé dishes or timbale molds. These are basically one and the same. An excellent source for these molds, along with other cooking equipment, is Bridge Kitchenware in New York City. Call toll free 1-800-BRIDGEK (274-3435). A large assortment of molds, soufflé dishes, pastry forms, etc. opens up endless possibilities for creativity in the kitchen and adds to the joy of cooking. I collect small pastry forms and have found it to be an addictive hobby.

PASTRY BAG: This is one of my favorite toys. Buy the largest pastry bag you can find with changeable tips. The basic tips include plain round, fluted, and star shaped. It's nice to have several sizes.

MISCELLANEOUS TOOLS: Every serious cook should have a set of good knives (chef's knife in two sizes, boning knife, and several paring knives), kitchen shears, a mallet for flattening meat, wooden spoons and wire whisks, a strainer and colander, spatulas, pastry brushes, and tweezers for removing small bones from fish.

Menu Suggestions

I hope these suggestions will help you in creating memorable meals.

— FALL —

Homecoming Game Lunch

Corn Chowder	*Beaujolais Louis Jadot*
Sausage in Crust	*J. Vidal Fleur Côte du Rhone*
Curly Endive Salad	
Purée of White Beans and Potatoes	
Lemon Custard Tart	

Christening Brunch

Tiny Cheese Tarts	*Champagne Brut Rosé*
Game Pie	*Julienas Duboeuf or*
or	*Jadot Beaujolais Cru*
Piperade (Sautéed Peppers & Scrambled Eggs)	
Green Salad	
Pear Tart	

Day of the Dead

Shrimp Quesadillas	*Gunderloch Riesling Dry (Rheinhessen)*
Poblanos Santa Fe	*or Zaca Mesa Roussane (Santa Barbara)*
Salmon with Red Pepper and Black Bean Sauce	
Pasta with Corn and Red Pepper	
Zucchini Timbales with Cumin	
Strawberry Ice Peppers	

Menu Featuring Game

Clam and Potato Soup	*Côtes du Rhone Blanc*
Venison Racks with Dried Cherry Sauce	*Hermitage (Northern Rhone)*
Potato Napoleons	
Creamed Spinach	
Chocolate Soufflé with Chocolate Surprise	

Thanksgiving

Spiced Pecans	*Carneros Creek Chardonnay (Carneros)*
Venison Pâté	*Stonestreet Pinot Noir (Sonoma)*
Wild Rice Soup	
Traditional Turkey and Dressing	
Cream Gravy	
Mashed Potatoes	
Honey Glazed Carrots	
Relish Tray	
Apple Pie and Pecan Pie	

ALTERNATIVE THANKSGIVING

Black Bean Soup with Sherry	*Talbot Chardonnay (Monterey)*
Turkey Roulade	*Grgich Hill Cabernet Sauvignon(Napa)*
Gravy	
Corn Pudding	
Potatoes au Gratin	
Green Beans Country Style	
Macadamia Nut Pie	

CHRISTMAS LUNCH

Cream of Brie Soup	*Jadot Meursault 1er Cru (Burgundy)*
Perfect Roast Beef	*Bouchard Pommard 1 er Cru (Côte d'Or)*
Tomato Tart	
Macaroni and Cheese	
Cornucopias with Lemon Cream	

FANCY LOW-FAT AFTER THE HOLIDAYS

Red Bell Pepper Soup	*Wild Horse Pinot Blanc (Central Coast)*
Chicken Parmigiana	*Ridge Lyton Springs Zinfandel (Sonoma)*
Green Beans with Red and Yellow Peppers	
Rice Pilaf	
Strawberry Sorbet with Raspberry Sauce and Fresh Berries	

— W I N T E R —

NEW YEAR'S EVE

Scallion Crêpes with Caviar	*Veuve Clicquot La Grande Dame*
Coquille St. Jacques	*Château La Nerthe (Châteauneuf-du-Pape)*
Steak au Poivre	
Fresh Asparagus with Hollandaise	
Potatoes Anna	
Floating Island	

ITALIAN DINNER BY THE FIRE

Prosciutto and Asparagus Roll-Ups	*Pinot Grigio Felluga (Collio)*
Veal Chop with Red Pepper Sauce	*Monsanto Chianti Classico Riserva (Tuscany)*
Garlic Custards	
Zucchini, Red Pepper, and Potato Gratin	
Crème Brûlée	

Valentine Dinner

Rigatoni with Chicken Mousse	*Taittinger Rosé Brut (France)*
Swordfish with Yellow Pepper Sauce	*Girard Chardonnay (Napa Valley)*
Rice with Zucchini Band	
Fresh Spinach	
Heart-Shaped Frozen Lemon Tower	
with Raspberry Sauce	

Special Occasion Buffet

Garlic Shrimp Hors d'oeuvres	*Trefethen Chardonnay (Napa Valley)*
Beef Tenderloin with Green Peppercorn Sauce	*Carneros Creek Pinot Noir (Carneros)*
Large Stuffed Mushrooms	
Kathryn's Potatoes	
Fresh Asparagus Vinaigrette	
Oreo Cheesecake	

Casual Super Bowl Dinner

Grilled Shrimp and White Bean Soup	*Napa Ridge Chardonnay (California)*
Pork Loin with Marsala	*DeLoach Zinfandel (Sonoma)*
Chard, Tomato, and Cheese Casserole	
Polenta Fritters	
Cream Cheese Crêpes with Apricot Sauce	

Anniversary Celebration

Ricotta Ravioli with Fall Vegetables	*Santa Margherita Pinot Grigio (Italy)*
Pork Tenderloin with Mustard Cream	*Cambria Pinot Noir (Santa Barbara)*
Wild Mushrooms in Puff Pastry Boxes	
Green Beans with Red and Yellow Peppers	
Chocolate Soufflé with Chocolate Surprise	

Special Guest Dinner

Watercress Soup	*Rosemount Semillon (Australia)*
Chicken with Gorgonzola	*M. Chiarlo Barolo (Piedmont)*
Two Potato Cake	
Red Pepper Timbale	
Frozen Blackberry and	
White Chocolate Mousse	

Lunch with a Southwestern Flair

Smoked Turkey, Avocado and	
Black Bean Roulade	
Red Corn and Chile Crusted Redfish	*Robert Eymael Riesling Kabinett (Mosel)*
Fideo	*Mantanzas Creek Sauvignon Blanc (Sonoma)*
Shredded Zucchini	
French Lace Cookie Tacos	

—SPRING—

GARDEN LUNCHEON

Crawfish Gazpacho   *Torres Viña Sol (Barcelona)*
Chicken with Ricotta and Fresh Tomatoes   *Montecillo Rioja (Spain)*
Four Grain Dressing
Green Salad with Edible Spring Flowers
Swiss Cheese Bread
Tiny Lemon Tarts

EASTER LUNCH

Shrimp and Scallop Terrine   *French Chablis 1 er Cru*
Lamb Racks with Rosemary   *Château Leoville-Barton (St. Julien)*
Polenta with Four Cheeses
Green Beans with Red and Yellow Peppers
Frozen Lemon Tower

COME WATCH THE ACADEMY AWARDS

Sausage in Crust with Dijon Mustard   *Monterey Pinot Blanc (Monterey)*
Sautéed Chicken with Calvados   *Mirassou Pinot Noir (Monterey)*
Garlic Buttered Noodles
Red Pepper Timbale
Lime Pie

FIESTA COCKTAIL PARTY

Quesadillas   *Chateau Ste. Michelle Johannisberg*
Miniature Flautas   *Riesling (Washington State)*
Guacamole   *Ponzi Pinot Noir (Oregon)*
Homemade Chips with Two Sauces
Corn and Green Chile Tamales

OUTDOOR LUNCH ON A COOL DAY

Concha Soup   *B.V. Gamay Beaujolais (California)*
Big Green Salad   *Ravenswood Zinfandel (Sonoma)*
Homemade Chips
Pepperidge Farm Cookies

GRADUATION CELEBRATION

Bacon Wrapped Scallops with Tartar Sauce   *Domaine Carneros Brut Champagne (Carneros)*
Lamb Loin with Marsala   *Château Montelena Cabernet Sauvignon (Napa)*
Wild Mushrooms in Puff Pastry Boxes
Spinach Timbale with Gorgonzola
on Fresh Spinach
Oreo Cheesecake

Spring Buffet for 100

Tiny Cheese Tarts   *Anselmi Soave Classico (Veneto)*
Salmon with Pesto   *Villa Mt. Eden Chardonnay (California)*
Fettuccine Alfredo
Asparagus and Sautéed Red Peppers,
cut into 2-inch pieces
Glamorous Chocolate Mousse Cake

Engagement Celebration

Warm Shrimp and Scallop Terrine with   *Cambria Chardonnay Reserve (Santa Barbara)*
Champagne Sauce   *Fess Parker Pinot Noir (Santa Barbara)*
Crown of Pork with Port Wine Sauce
Mushroom Strudel with Kale and
Red Peppers
Great Northern Beans with
Zucchini and Carrots
Banana Napoleons

— S U M M E R —

Before the Heat Country French Dinner

French Onion Soup   *Tavel Rosé (Rhone)*
Roasted Chicken with Basil or Tarragon   *Chinon (Loire)*
Curly Endive Salad
Leeks au Gratin
Two Tone Bread
Free Form Apple Tart

I Miss My Friends, Let's Get Together

Shrimp Toast   *Sancerre Michel Redde (Loire)*
Pork with Sesame Seeds   *Georges Duboeuf Côtes de Rhone*
Couscous with Peas and Red Peppers
Adelaide's Squash
Sorbet in Cookie Cups

Bridge Luncheon

Carrot Soup with Ginger   *Bernardus Chardonnay (Monterey)*
Chicken Salad with Blue Cheese
Millet Bread
Crème Brûlée

Father's Day Bar-B-Que

Scallops in Bacon with Tartar Sauce
Grilled Lamb Chops Cajun Style
Succotash
Parmesan Grits
Green Salad
Hush Puppies
Peach Cobbler

Fall Creek Granite Reserve (Texas)
Hess Collection Cabernet Sauvignon (Napa)

Fourth of July

Popcorn
Game Hens on the Grill
Country Style Green Beans
Creamed Fresh Corn
Cornbread in Cast Iron Skillet
Kathryn's Pecan Pie

Wild Horse Pinot Noir (Central Coast)
Zaca Mesa Syrah (Santa Barbara)

Kitchen Shower

Prosciutto and Asparagus Roll Ups
Pasta Shells with Ricotta and Basil
Tomato Sauce
Green Salad
Foccacia
Lemon Custard Tart

Chalone Chardonnay (Pinnacles)

Welcome to Town

Scallion Crêpes
Potato Basket Filled with Mixed Greens
Seafood Sausage with Red Pepper Vinaigrette
Millet Bread
French Lace Cookies

Kendall Jackson Pinot Noir (California)

Light Supper for Childhood Friends

Carrot Soup with Ginger
Pasta with Dove Topping
Buttered White Bread
Salad with Tomato, Avocado, and
Mango Slices
Apple Pie with Ice Cream

Gunderloch Kabinett Jean Baptiste (Rheinhessen)

Appetizers

Caviar Mold   12

Bacon Wrapped Scallops   13
Tartar Sauce

Tiny Cheese Tarts   14

Chicken Liver Mousse en Gelée   15

Smoked Turkey, Avocado, and Black Bean Roulade *   16

Miniature Flautas with Two Sauces   17
Tomatillo Salsa *
Roasted Tomato Salsa *

Homemade Toasted Tortilla Chips   19

Shrimp Toast   20

Stuffed Mushrooms   21

Prosciutto and Asparagus Roll-Ups   22

Scallion Crêpes with Caviar   23

Broiled Garlic Shrimp   24

Shrimp Quesadillas   25

Venison Pâté   26

denotes a low fat dish

Caviar Mold

SERVES 20-25

*This dish is always a hit. It can be made several days ahead, is great
for large parties, and looks beautiful on a coffee or buffet table.
If, for some reason, guests are not circulating, spread cream cheese
and caviar on crackers and pass on a tray.*

6 8-ounce packages
   Philadelphia cream cheese,
   room temperature
Juice of 4 lemons
2 teaspoons salt
1-2 cups sour cream
4 hard-boiled eggs, peeled
   and chopped
4 green onions, chopped

MOLD: Put half of cream cheese, lemon juice, salt and sour cream in food processor. Process until smooth. Spread mixture into 9-inch spring form pan. Process remaining half of the same ingredients and reserve. Chop eggs. Spread half on top of cream cheese mixture in spring form pan. Reserve other half for decoration. Chop green onion. Use some dark green stem for color. Sprinkle half of green onion on top of egg. Cover with reserved cream cheese mixture. Smooth top layer of cream cheese. Cover with plastic wrap. Refrigerate several hours or overnight.

1 2-ounce jar black caviar
Hard-boiled egg, chopped
Tomato rose
Fresh parsley

GARNISH: Wash black caviar in small strainer. Drain well. Place ring mold with cream cheese on serving dish. Remove sides of ring mold. Arrange 1-inch ring of caviar around outer edge of mold. Next to caviar ring, add ring of chopped egg, then ring of green onion. Fill small center with additional caviar. Place some parsley or tomato rose in center. Cover with plastic wrap and refrigerate.

TO SERVE: Remove plastic wrap. If desired, surround with parsley. Serve with crackers.

VARIATION: To create a different look, use a heart shaped mold. Line entire mold with plastic wrap. Fill mold in same manner. Refrigerate several hours or overnight. To unmold, turn mold over onto serving dish. Remove mold and plastic wrap. Smooth top and sides. Decorate top half side of heart with red caviar . Decorate other side with chopped green onion.

NOTE: It is necessary to wash inexpensive black caviar to remove black dye. Otherwise, caviar will turn white cream cheese an ugly grey color.

Bacon Wrapped Scallops
Tartar Sauce

SERVES 6-8

*This is one of the world's best taste treats. It has been in my family
for a long, long time. I credit my mother, Katie Wood, with this
tartar sauce. It is the easiest and the best. Serve it with
any fried fish or shellfish.*

1 cup flour, seasoned with salt
  and pepper
1 tablespoon paprika
1 teaspoon garlic powder
2 eggs, lightly beaten
1 cup fresh bread crumbs
1 pound sea scallops, cut in half
Salt and pepper
12 bacon strips, cut in half

BACON WRAPPED SCALLOPS: Preheat oven to 400°F. Combine seasoned flour with paprika and garlic powder. Place in mixing bowl. Place eggs and bread crumbs in separate mixing bowls. Wash and dry scallops. Season with salt and pepper. Coat each scallop piece in flour, then in egg, then in bread crumbs. Wrap each breaded scallop in 1/2 strip of bacon. Secure with toothpick. Place on baking sheet. Bake until bacon is crisp and scallops are cooked through, approximately 25 minutes.

2 large dill pickles, diced
1/2 cup diced yellow onion
2 cups mayonnaise
Juice of one lemon

TARTAR SAUCE: Combine pickles, onion, mayonnaise and lemon juice in mixing bowl.

TO SERVE: Serve scallops hot. Pass on tray with small bowl of tartar sauce.

VARIATION: Bread whole, button mushrooms exactly as you would the scallops. Omit bacon. Deep fry in hot oil until crisp. Serve with tartar sauce for a great taste treat.

NOTES: These can be assembled several hours before serving. Bake at last minute. They may be reheated in 350°F oven for 10 minutes.

Tiny Cheese Tarts

MAKES 24-30 SMALL TARTS

This recipe came from a friend in San Antonio who served them to me at a dinner in her home. I felt they were truly impressive. The tarts can be eaten in one bite, which makes them great cocktail fare. I use them often when catering. The shells may be made ahead and frozen and the filling may be prepared several days before serving.

1 sheet of Pillsbury pie crust
1 2-inch round to be used to cut dough
1-inch tart shell molds

TART SHELLS: Roll Pillsbury dough out slightly. Using 2-inch round cutter, cut dough into rounds. Press cut out round between two small 1-inch tart molds. (These are available in good cooking stores such as Williams-Sonoma.) Bake tart molds in preheated 400°F oven for 20 minutes. It is not necessary to remove top molds until shells are completely baked. Once baked, remove from molds and cool. Shells may be used immediately or frozen at this point.

1/2 cup mayonnaise
1 cup grated Swiss cheese
1/2 cup grated Parmesan cheese
Pickled jalapeños, seeded and cut into small shapes
Salt (optional)

FILLING: Combine mayonnaise, Swiss cheese, and Parmesan cheese in food processor. Process until well combined, about 30 seconds. Cut pickled jalapeños into stars with small aspic cutter.

TO ASSEMBLE: Place teaspoon of filling into each tart shell. Place jalapeño star in center. Broil under hot broiler until browned and bubbling, about 2-3 minutes. Season with salt if desired.

TO SERVE: Pass on serving tray. Best served immediately after broiling.

VARIATION: The idea of using mayonnaise to bind ingredients is an old one. Use your imagination. Change filling to mayonnaise, onion, parsley and cheese. Bake on toasted bread rounds. Or make a filling of chopped black olives, cheddar cheese, curry, and mayonnaise and broil on English muffins. Cut in quarters to serve. If jalapeño stars are too much trouble, cut them into small cubes. Also consider cutting shapes out of roasted red peppers.

NOTE: For this recipe, Pillsbury dough is better than homemade. My basic recipe for pastry has so much butter and is so light that tarts tend to break easily.

Chicken Liver Mousse en Gelée

Serves 8-10

Working with gelatin to decorate patés or mousses can be extremely creative. Some wonderful tasting gelatins are sold at specialty cooking stores, but for your first attempt, Knox unflavored gelatin will work fine.

1 pound chicken livers
1/2 cup milk
2 tablespoons butter
1 clove garlic, chopped
1/2 small onion, chopped
2 tablespoons flour
1 cup milk
3 large eggs
2 large egg yolks
1 teaspoon salt
1/2 teaspoon white pepper
1/3 cup heavy cream
1/4 cup Madeira
2 tablespoons cognac

MOUSSE: Soak livers in 1/2 cup milk for 20 minutes to remove bitterness. Preheat oven to 325°F. Oil loaf pan or spray with a non-stick cooking spray and set aside. Melt butter in medium saucepan. Add garlic and onion. Cook until tender, but not browned, about 2 minutes. Add flour and cook 1 minute. Add 1 cup milk and whisk until smooth. Bring to boil and continue whisking until mixture is thick. Cool to room temperature. Reserve. Place in food processor and purée until smooth. Pat livers dry. Add to food processor with cream sauce. Process until smooth. Add eggs, yolks, seasonings and process again until very smooth. Add cream, Madeira and cognac. Process until smooth again. Strain. Pour mixture into prepared mold. Bake, uncovered, in water bath, until knife inserted comes out clean. This should take about 50 minutes. Unmold and place in refrigerator until chilled. Smooth top and sides.

1/4 cup chicken broth
1 package gelatin
1/4 cup chicken broth

Thinly sliced green onion stems
Roasted red bell pepper
Fresh herb leaves

GELÉE: Dissolve gelatin in 1/4 cup broth. Let harden. Heat gelatin with additional 1/4 cup broth until all gelatin is dissolved. Using a pastry brush, lightly brush gelatin onto cold, smooth mousse. Refrigerate 15 minutes. Dip vegetables you are using for decoration in warm gelatin. Place on top of first layer of gelée. Use a pastry brush to add another layer of gelatin. Refrigerate 15 minutes or until hard. Continue adding gelatin until you have a nice coating on vegetables. Place mousse in refrigerator after each application of gelatin to harden quickly.

TO SERVE: Serve with crackers of choice.

NOTE: To make Hot Chicken Liver Mousse, follow directions for mousse, but bake in individual molds in 300°F oven for 30 minutes. Unmold in au gratin dishes. Serve napped with a cream sauce and fresh, chopped chives. Sauce: 3 cups heavy cream and 1 tablespoon Bovril, reduced over high heat until thick, about 10-15 minutes. A great first course!

Smoked Turkey, Avocado and Black Bean Roulade on Whole Wheat Tortilla

This is a recipe that was given to me by a friend. It is a wonderful, low fat hors d'oeurve with many possible variations.

---

1 15-ounce can black beans, drained
4 ounces light cream cheese, softened
4-6 garlic cloves, peeled and minced
1 teaspoon ground cumin
1 cup cilantro, chopped
2 serrano peppers, seeded and chopped
14 whole wheat tortillas
2 red bell peppers, diced
1 red onion, diced
2 avocados, diced
14 slices smoked turkey

ROULADE: Put black beans, cream cheese, garlic, cumin, cilantro, and serrano peppers in processor. Process until smooth. Spread black bean mixture on very fresh whole wheat tortillas. Combine red bell pepper, onion and avocado. Sprinkle 1-2 tablespoons on top of black bean mixture. Top with one slice smoked turkey. Roll tightly, like a cigar. Tightly wrap tortillas rolls in plastic wrap. Chill 2 hours or overnight.

TO SERVE: Remove plastic wrap. Slice on the diagonal into bite size pieces and serve cold.

VARIATION: Use flour tortillas. Spread with cream cheese seasoned with lemon juice, salt, and pepper. Sprinkle on capers, chopped egg, chopped onion, and dill. Lay smoked salmon on top. Roll up and chill.

Miniature Flautas
Tomatillo Salsa
Roasted Tomato Salsa

SERVES 8-10

*Friends from Mexico brought this traditional fare with them when
they moved to San Antonio. After I raved about them, they were
kind enough to invite me into their kitchen where Rosa, their
marvelous cook, taught me the secrets of flautas. The sauces are
good served alone with homemade tortilla chips.
Both sauces are very low in fat.*

2 chicken breasts
Water or canned broth,
   seasoned with celery, parsley,
   onion, thyme, oregano, salt
   and pepper
2 tablespoons vegetable oil
1/2 cup finely chopped onion
2 cloves garlic, chopped
1 10-ounce can diced tomatoes
   and green chiles (Ro-Tel),
   drained
Salt and pepper to taste
Reserved chicken

FILLING: Boil breasts in seasoned water or canned chicken broth until done, approximately 20 minutes. Remove meat from bone and shred finely. Reserve. Heat vegetable oil in small saucepan. Cook onion and garlic in oil over moderately high heat until vegetables are soft. Add tomatoes and green chiles. Cook until most of moisture has evaporated. This will take at least 30 minutes. Season with salt and pepper. Add reserved chicken. Allow to cool.

12 corn tortillas, very thin
3 cups vegetable oil
Toothpicks

FLAUTAS: Heat 1/2-inch of oil in small sauté pan until hot but not smoking. Dip tortillas, one at a time, in hot oil for approximately 10-15 seconds or until just softened. Set aside to drain. You may stack softened tortillas on one plate.

2 tablespoons vegetable oil
6 large tomatillos
2 serrano peppers
1 cup cilantro, stems removed
1 piece of onion
Salt to taste

TOMATILLO SALSA: Heat oil in a comal or heavy cast iron skillet. (A comal is a flat cast iron plate used throughout Mexico.) Remove shucks from tomatillos. Wash well. (Tomatillos are slightly sticky when shucks are removed.) Place washed tomatillos and serranos onto hot, oiled skillet or comal. Cook over moderately high heat until very charred. When charred, put serrano peppers into cold water. Remove as much skin as possible from serrano peppers. Place charred and unpeeled tomatillos, serrano

continued on next page

peppers, cilantro and onion in blender or food processor. Add some water, 1/4-1/2 cup, if necessary, and purée. Season with salt.

---

2 tablespoons vegetable oil
2 large red tomatoes, cut in
   half horizontally
1 large garlic clove, peeled
1 teaspoon salt

ROASTED TOMATO SALSA: Lightly oil cast iron skillet or comal. Place tomatoes on skillet or comal, cut side down. Cook over moderately high heat until tomatoes are charred and very tender. Turn over. Char other side. Remove peel. Put tomatoes in blender or food processor. Add garlic and salt. Blend until smooth.

TO ASSEMBLE: Place one tablespoon of chicken filling in each soft tortilla. Roll up tightly. Spear filled tortilla in three places with toothpicks. Repeat process adding next two filled tortillas to original one. Place tortillas on toothpicks so that openings touch each other. You will end up with three filled tortillas tightly grouped together. Cut into thirds. Fry in hot oil. Serve immediately.

TO SERVE: Remove toothpicks from flautas. Pass on serving tray with choice of red and green sauces.

VARIATION: *Shrimp, crab, sausage, etc. may be substituted for chicken.*

NOTES: *Once flautas are put together, and before they are fried, they may be put into sealable plastic bags and frozen. Defrost before frying. Be sure to buy corn tortillas labeled "very thin."*

Homemade Toasted Tortilla Chips

These chips are, perhaps, the first item I ever learned to cook.
They are just as popular today as they were years ago. Serve them
with salsa of your choice.

6 cups vegetable oil
1 package corn tortillas,
   10 per package
Salt

CHIPS: Heat vegetable oil in 3-quart sauté pan until very hot but not smoking. Cut tortillas into quarters. Drop into hot oil. Fry until crisp and brown. Oil will stop bubbling when chips are ready. Drain in bowl lined with paper towels. Salt generously while still warm.

TO SERVE: Serve immediately or freeze. These freeze beautifully. They do not need to be defrosted before using. Reheating chips in preheated 350°F oven for approximately 5 minutes always makes them nicer. They go straight from freezer to oven.

NOTE: You must fry tortillas in HOT oil or they will absorb too much oil and taste greasy.

Shrimp Toast

SERVES 6-8

Shrimp toast is a classic. It is easy and quite magical as the shrimp toast is fried upside down, yet never loses its topping.

1/2 pound shrimp, peeled
1 teaspoon grated ginger
1/4 cup minced green onion
1 large egg white
1 tablespoon soy sauce
2 cloves garlic, minced
1-2 teaspoons sesame oil
2 tablespoons water chestnuts, minced
Pepperidge Farm very thin white bread
Vegetable oil for frying
Parsley for garnish

SHRIMP TOAST: Peel and devein shrimp. Put in food processor with ginger, green onion, egg white, soy sauce, garlic, sesame oil, and water chestnuts and purée. Cut crusts off bread. Cut bread twice on the diagonal to make 4 small triangles. Spread 1 teaspoon shrimp filling on each bread triangle. Place parsley leaf on top of filling. Fry, shrimp side down, in several inches of hot vegetable oil until brown, about 2-3 minutes. Drain on paper towels. May turn to fry bottom if desired.

TO SERVE: Serve immediately.

NOTE: These would be good served with Jezebel sauce, found on page 100.

Stuffed Mushrooms

For hors d'oeuvres, use the smallest button mushrooms you can find. Turn this into a side vegetable by using the largest button mushrooms available.

....

8 ounces whole button mushrooms

1/2-3/4 stick butter, melted

MUSHROOMS: Wipe whole mushroom caps with paper towel to remove excess dirt. Do not wash. Remove stems. Reserve. Brush caps with melted butter. Place on baking sheet.

....

4 green onions, minced
Reserved mushroom stems
2 tablespoons butter
2 tablespoons flour
1/2 cup heavy cream
3 tablespoons parsley, minced
Salt and pepper

FILLING: Put green onion and mushroom stems in food processor. Mince. Melt 2 tablespoons butter in small saucepan. Add onion-mushroom mixture. Cook mixture over moderate heat until most of moisture has evaporated. This will take longer than you think, about 20 minutes. Add flour. Cook 1 minute. Add cream. Cook mixture, stirring occasionally, until thickened, about 2-3 minutes. Add parsley. Season with salt and pepper to taste.

....

1/2 cup grated Swiss cheese

TO ASSEMBLE: Place 1 teaspoon filling in buttered mushroom caps. Top with grated cheese. If not serving immediately, cover with plastic wrap and refrigerate. These may be assembled the day before serving.

TO SERVE: Preheat broiler. Broil 2-3 minutes or until cheese is melted and brown. Place on serving tray. Remember to use smallest mushrooms possible. Allow 2 per person.

VARIATION: Use any combination of wild mushrooms.

NOTE: I have served these for large buffet dinners as a side vegetable using large mushrooms, and they are extremely popular. This dish is quite expensive, so allow only 1 1/2 to 2 mushrooms per person. If you run out, it will be because they were so wonderful.

Prosciutto and Asparagus Roll-Ups

SERVES 4

In all of my reading, studying, and creating new recipes, I find that discovering new hors d'oeurves is one of the most difficult. I credit the inspiration for this appetizer to Daniel Boulud, owner of Daniel Restaurant in New York. It is excellent.

Salted water
2 large asparagus spears
1 sheet of phyllo from
    purchased package
1/4 stick melted butter, cooled
2 thin slices prosciutto
Dijon mustard

ROLL-UPS: Bring pot of salted water to boil. Add asparagus. Cook until crisp-tender, about 5 minutes. Refresh under ice cold water. Drain. Remove one sheet of phyllo from package. Using pastry brush, coat lightly with cooled, melted butter. Lay two slices of prosciutto down width of phyllo, along side closest to yourself and coat lightly with Dijon mustard. Lay two asparagus spears on top of prosciutto. Tip of one will touch bottom of other. Roll phyllo tightly around prosciutto-asparagus pieces, as you would roll a cigarette. Refrigerate, covered with plastic wrap or bake immediately in preheated 350°F oven for 10 minutes, or until phyllo is crisp. These roll-ups can also be frozen. When crisp, cut on diagonal into bite size pieces, about 8 per roll.

NOTES: I found it is easiest to cut phyllo into bite-size pieces before baking. However, if you are planning to freeze them, freeze in one long roll. Cut when defrosted but before baking. A non-stick cooking spray may be used instead of butter. Of course, you lose some flavor. At Daniel Restaurant, the chef used white asparagus instead of green. Choose the largest asparagus you can find.

Scallion Crêpes with Caviar

SERVES 25-30

Although crêpes go in and out of style, the technique is still very important. Crêpes serve as a basis for creating a variety of modern dishes. This recipe was included by popular request from my students.

1 tablespoon melted butter,
   cooled
1 cup flour
1/2 teaspoon salt
2 eggs
3/4 cup milk
1/2 cup chopped green onions
   (use some of the dark green)

CRÊPES: Put butter, flour, salt, and eggs in food processor. Process to combine, about 5-10 seconds. With machine running, pour milk through feed tube. Scrape sides. This should take no more than 1 minute. Transfer batter to bowl. Stir in green onion. Butter crêpe pan or small skillet. Spoon batter into pan by tablespoons. Be sure to pick up some onion in each spoonful. Pan should be hot but not smoking. Make crêpes about 1 1/2 to 2-inches in diameter. Batter is thicker than most crêpe batters, so it will not spread out when added to sauté pan. This will enable you to use a larger skillet and make 5-6 small crêpes at a time. Cook crêpes over moderately high heat until lightly browned. Turn. Cook only several seconds on bottom side. Mini-crêpes can be used immediately or frozen. Frozen crêpes should be defrosted and reheated in 300°F oven for 10 minutes before serving. Wrap in foil to reheat. Batter will make 30-50 crêpes.

4 ounces cream cheese,
   room temperature
2 tablespoons sour cream
1-2 tablespoons heavy cream
Salt to taste
Juice of 1/2 lemon
1 green onion, chopped

FILLING: Put cream cheese, sour cream, heavy cream, salt, lemon juice, and green onion in food processor. Process until smooth.

Small jar of red caviar

TO ASSEMBLE AND SERVE: Place 1/2 teaspoon cream cheese mixture onto each crêpe. Fold over. Place 1/4 teaspoon red caviar on top of each folded crêpe. Caviar should be visible. Place on tray and serve.

Broiled Garlic Shrimp

SERVES 6

*Garlic shrimp was the only appetizer served at Morton's Restaurant
in San Antonio at a friend's 50th birthday party. I thought it was
fabulous, so here is my version. When serving shrimp as an hors
d'oeuvre you will never have enough. Plan on 2-3 per person.
Guests always consider shrimp a real treat.*

1 pound medium shrimp
Salt and freshly ground
   black pepper
1 stick butter, melted
3-5 cloves garlic, minced
2-3 cups fresh bread crumbs

SHRIMP: Peel and devein shrimp. Leave tails on if you desire. Season with salt and freshly ground black pepper. Melt butter in small saucepan. Add minced garlic. The amount you use will depend on how much garlic you like. Sauté 2-3 minutes over moderately low heat or until garlic is soft. Cool to room temperature. Make bread crumbs out of any white bread. Simply tear bread into pieces and put into food processor. Process bread into crumbs, about 30 seconds. Do not toast or dry out. Make more than needed for they can be frozen. Do not substitute canned bread crumbs. Coat shrimp first with butter-garlic mixture, then with bread crumbs. Place on baking sheet. Broil shrimp until browned, about 2 minutes per side.

TO SERVE: Serve immediately. Pass on a platter decorated with your choice of fresh herbs.

NOTES: *Peel shrimp, melt butter and garlic, make bread crumbs a day ahead. Bread shrimp one hour before guests come. You will then have a seemingly effortless hors'd oeuvre. Make bread crumbs out of any white bread, even old hot dog buns will work. Do not dry out if using for breading.*

Shrimp Quesadillas

Quesadillas of all types are always popular. They are easy to make and offer almost unlimited possibilities for creativity in the kitchen. The shrimp in this recipe can be changed to anything from chicken to beef to chiles. Add cilantro. Add tomatoes. The only rule is to use plenty of grated cheese. The cheese is the glue that binds the two tortillas together to make the quesadilla.

1 pound shrimp
1 1/2 cups grated Swiss or
  Monterey Jack cheese
1/3 cup chopped green chiles,
  canned
6 large flour tortillas
1-2 tablespoons butter per
  quesadilla, as needed

QUESADILLAS: Cook shrimp in boiling, salted water until done, about 1-2 minutes. Peel. Chop shrimp into 1/4-inch pieces. Combine shrimp, cheese, and green chiles. Place 3 flour tortillas on baking sheet. Sprinkle each tortilla with 1/3 shrimp, green chile, and cheese mixture. Top with another tortilla. Heat butter in large skillet. Add 1 quesadilla. Cook over moderately high heat until bottom is brown. While cooking, press top tortilla down with spatula to ensure that top and bottom stick together. Turn quesadilla over. Cook until brown on other side. Repeat with the remaining uncooked quesadillas.

TO SERVE: Cut quesadillas into wedges. Serve immediately. Quesadillas may be sautéed several hours ahead and reheated on a baking sheet in preheated 350°F oven. Serve with sour cream or guacamole.

VARIATION: Cut flour tortillas into 2-inch rounds. Put a combination of roasted garlic and cheese between layers. Make 4 layers. Sauté in same manner as this recipe. If not using immediately, place on baking sheet. Reheat in 350°F oven. This makes a nice side dish for a Southwestern meal. When making these individual quesadillas, don't press the layers down too tightly or you will have a flat dish. In this instance, you want a quesadilla with some height.

NOTE: You will need to wipe skillet clean with a paper towel and add new butter from time to time, if cooking many quesadillas, as butter tends to burn and must be replaced. Do not use olive oil. It will adversely affect the flavor.

Venison Pâté

SERVES 8-10

I introduced this recipe in one of my earliest classes. The inspiration came from a recipe booklet that accompanied my first Cuisinart. The original recipe used beef, but in Texas, many people have venison. This recipe allows one to use lesser cuts of venison, please the hunter in the family and delight guests.

4 cups cooked venison
1/4 cup olive oil
Salt and freshly ground pepper
1 2-ounce tin anchovies, drained
3-4 tablespoons capers
1 teaspoon garlic powder
1/2 cup chopped onion
2-3 sticks butter, room temper-
    ature, cut into tablespoons
Juice of 1 lemon
2 teaspoons salt
1 teaspoon pepper

PÂTÉ: Wash and dry venison. Remove any sinew or places that have freezer burn. Coat outside generously with olive oil. Season with salt and freshly ground pepper. Bake in preheated 350°F oven until done, about 15 minutes for a small piece of meat. Cut into cubes and place in food processor. Process until nicely chopped. (I would not suggest using backstrap. It is too good a cut of meat for this dish. Use ham if possible.) Add anchovies, capers, garlic powder, and onion to processor with venison. Process to combine. With machine running, add butter through feed tube. Add lemon juice, salt, and pepper. Process until mixture forms smooth ball.

TO ASSEMBLE: Mold pâté into a decorative shape or line a loaf pan with plastic wrap and fill with pâté mixture. If you use a loaf pan, chill pâté several hours or overnight before unmolding. I originally formed it into a pineapple, using pâté for the body and the top of a real pineapple as the top. Use sliced, pitted olives for "eyes" of pineapple. One of my more artistic students sculpted it into the form of a sleeping cat. The pâté holds its shape very well, so you may use any mold. (See page 117 where I used a chocolate mold to shape pâté into form of a chicken.)

TO SERVE: Unmold. Let sit outside the refrigerator at least 1 hour before serving. Butter must soften so pâté will have a texture that is easy to spread. Serve with crackers.

VARIATION: Beef, pork or any combination of meats may be used to change this dish. You may also want to add additional herbs of your choice.

NOTE: Be sure not to cook meat at too high a temperature. This could cause outside of meat to form a crust. If this happens, pâté will never be smooth. If some crunchy parts do form, cut them off before processing. Pâté may be frozen.

Soups

Black Bean Soup * 28

Clam and Potato Soup 29

Carrot Soup with Ginger * 30

Concha Soup 31

Cream of Corn Chowder 32

Crawfish Gazpacho * 33

Red Bell Pepper Soup * 34

Watercress Soup 35

Shrimp Gumbo * 36

Grilled Shrimp and White Bean Soup 37

Spring Soup 38

Classic French Onion Soup 39

French Vegetable Soup * 40

Wild Rice Soup 41

Cream of Brie 42

* denotes a low fat dish

Black Bean Soup

SERVES 4-6

There are many recipes for black bean soup; however, I feel this one is better and more interesting than many I have tried. The Madeira, lemon, rice, and egg garnish give it a European flavor.

1 pound black beans, or 2 cups
3-6 cups water
3-6 cups beef broth
1 ham hock, split
1 onion, chopped
3 teaspoons dried red peppers, crushed
2 cloves
1 bay leaf
Salt
Tabasco

BEANS: Sort through beans with your hands. There are small rocks among them. Wash beans well. Do not soak overnight. Put beans in stock pot with enough water and broth to cover beans. Add ham hock, onion, dried red peppers, cloves, and bay leaf. Bring to a boil, then reduce heat to simmer. Cook 2-3 hours or until beans are tender. You must continue to add broth and water to keep beans covered. As beans cook, the liquid tends to cook away. Remove ham hock and bay leaf. Purée beans in blender, adding additional stock if necessary to reach desired consistency. Add enough broth to create desired soup consistency. Season with salt and Tabasco. Be generous with the salt. You may need to add lots of additional broth. Add enough to make beans a "soup."

1/4 cup Madeira
1 lemon, sliced into thin rounds
1 hard boiled egg, sliced
Rice, cooked
1 green onion, sliced

TO ASSEMBLE AND SERVE: Before serving, reheat soup with Madeira. Serve in large tureen. Float lemon slices and hard boiled egg slices on top. Serve bowls of rice and green onion on side. These can be spooned into soup by each individual.

VARIATION: To make this a Southwest dish, forget the rice, Madeira, etc. Instead, season soup with 2 tablespoons cumin while beans are cooking. Add chopped cilantro. Thin down sour cream with milk. Use a fork to "throw" it decoratively on top of soup.

NOTES: If you are on a strictly no fat diet, you must eliminate ham hock. Soup will still be wonderful, but it's definitely better with ham. Soup can be frozen. A fun luncheon would be to serve only soup with salad and bread. Have a little Madeira, rice, and onion at each place.

Clam and Potato Soup

SERVES 6

This recipe, given to me by a dear family friend years ago, is one the easiest and best soups ever. It is especially good in winter.

---

2 10-ounce cans potato soup
2 cups half and half cream
1 4-ounce can minced clams
1/2 package frozen white shoe peg corn, defrosted
Salt and freshly ground black pepper

SOUP: Process potato soup with half and half in food processor or blender. Add additional cream or milk if needed to thin soup. Stir in clams and shoe peg corn. Season with salt and pepper to taste.

1/4 cup chopped parsley

TO SERVE: Heat soup. Sprinkle top with parsley.

Carrot Soup with Ginger

Serves 4-6

This useful soup can be served hot or cold. The ginger gives it a fresh taste and guests will never suspect it is low fat.

5 cups chicken broth
2 cups carrots cut into
   1-inch pieces
1 cup chopped potato
1/3-1/2 cup chicken broth
1 1/2 tablespoons peeled and
   minced ginger root
2 cloves garlic, minced
1 cup onion, minced
Additional broth
Salt and pepper or
   Tabasco to taste
1/2 cup cream, optional

SOUP: Place 5 cups broth in 3-quart sauté pan. Add carrots and potatoes. Bring to a boil. Reduce heat. Simmer until vegetables are tender, about 15 minutes. After cooking potatoes and carrots, you will have approximately 3 cups broth remaining. Cool. Reserve. In separate small saucepan, add additional 1/3 cup broth. Add minced ginger root, garlic, and onion. Sauté until tender. Watch carefully as broth could evaporate and cause vegetables to burn. If broth evaporates, add small amount of additional broth. When tender, combine with carrot-potato mixture. Place combined vegetables with broth in blender. Purée until smooth. Thin with additional broth if necessary to achieve desired consistency. You could need up to 1-2 cups broth. Season to taste. Use Tabasco if you do not want pepper to show in the soup.

1/3 cup chopped green onion
1/3 cup sour cream
1-2 tablespoons milk

TO SERVE: Serve hot or cold, topped with green onion. Include some dark green stem. Contrasting orange and green colors make a beautiful presentation. Thin down sour cream with milk. Put into plastic squeeze bottle and decorate top of soup.

NOTES: It is fun to serve carrot soup in the same bowl as Spring Soup. Sprinkle tiny bits of chopped green onion, cucumber and carrot on top. See photo on page 129. A blender works better in this recipe than a food processor.

Concha Soup

The recipe for this soup was inspired by a similar one served at
El Mirador Restaurant in San Antonio. I served this soup one cool
summer day in Aspen to a large crowd. We served it as picnic fare
with a big salad. Concha *is the Spanish word for shell.*

---

1 chicken
1 tablespoon dried basil
1 tablespoon dried oregano
1 tablespoon dried thyme
Salt and pepper
1/2 onion, roughly sliced
1 stalk celery, roughly chopped

CHICKEN AND STOCK: Wash chicken. Remove innards and excess fat. Put chicken in large pot and cover with water, seasoned with basil, oregano, thyme, salt, pepper, onion and celery. Bring seasoned water to boil. Reduce heat. Simmer chicken until done, about 45 minutes. Allow to cool in broth. If possible refrigerate overnight. When cold, fat from chicken will rise to surface and harden. It can easily be spooned off top. Remove chicken from stock. Remove meat from bone and cut into bite size pieces. Reserve chicken. Strain stock and save as base for soup.

3-4 cups vegetable oil
3 dried chiles anchos
8 tortillas, cut into 1/2-inch
    strips

ADDITIONS TO SOUP: Heat vegetable oil in small skillet until hot but not smoking. Seed and remove stems from chile anchos. Fry in hot oil for 30 seconds. Drain on paper towels. They will be very crisp. In same oil, fry tortilla strips 1-2 minutes or until oil stops bubbling and tortillas are crisp. Drain on paper towels. Reserve chips for garnish.

1/2 cup chicken stock
1 cup chopped onion
5 cloves garlic, chopped
1 28-ounce can whole tomatoes
Reserved fried chiles anchos
2 cups cilantro
Reserved stock, 8-10 cups
4 cups dried pasta shells
Reserved cooked chicken
1 pound fresh spinach,
    washed and cleaned
Salt and pepper

TO FINISH SOUP: Put 1/2 cup reserved chicken stock in small saucepan. Add onion and garlic. Sauté until tender. Purée tomatoes, fried chiles anchos, sautéed onion and garlic, and cilantro in blender. You will need to do this in several batches. Put 8-10 cups stock in large soup pot. Add puréed vegetables and dried pasta shells. Cook soup over moderately high heat until pasta is done. Pasta will absorb quite a bit of liquid. You may need to add more stock. Add reserved cooked chicken and fresh spinach. Correct seasoning. Spice up with Tabasco or picante sauce if desired. (If made ahead, you'll need to add much more broth before serving. Trust your instincts.)

1/2-1 cup grated Monterey
    Jack cheese
Reserved toasted tortillas

TO SERVE: Put soup in large tureen. Sprinkle top with Monterey Jack cheese and toasted tortilla chips.

Cream of Corn Chowder

SERVES 6-8

This is a wonderful winter soup. Great for cold weather picnics.

---

4 strips bacon
2 tablespoons bacon grease
1/4 cup chopped onion
4 cups frozen corn, defrosted
4 tablespoons butter
4 tablespoons flour
3 cups milk
1 cup light cream
Salt and pepper

CORN CHOWDER: Fry bacon until crisp in 3-quart sauté pan. Remove bacon from pan. Drain on paper towels and crumble into small pieces. Reserve. Pour out all but 2 tablespoons of grease. Add onion to bacon grease. Sauté until soft. Roughly chop corn in food processor. Add to onion. Cook over moderate heat until corn begins to lightly brown. Melt butter in same pan. Add flour and cook for 1-2 minutes. Be sure all flour is incorporated. Add milk. Turn heat to high and cook until thickened, stirring at all times with whisk. Add cream and reserved bacon. Season with salt and pepper.

TO SERVE: Reheat. Serve in large tureen, individual bowls or mugs.

VARIATION: Chopped and sautéed red bell peppers would add color and vary taste.

Crawfish Gazpacho

SERVES 6-8

*In 1982 I spent a week at Roger Verge's school in the South of France.
I stayed at the Grey d'Albion in Cannes, in which there was a Michelin
two star restaurant. A variation of this gazpacho was featured on
the menu. It was the first time I had seen our Texas guacamole
incorporated into a French menu. To me, it was an indication of the
mixing of many cuisines that lay ahead. As Madeleine Kamann
once told me, "All this blending of cuisines is made possible by the
airplane and its ability to transport fresh ingredients over continents."*

---

1 28-ounce can tomatoes
1/2 onion, cut into chunks
2 cloves garlic
Juice of 2 lemons
1/4 cup Pace Picante Sauce
1/2 cup cilantro
2-4 cups spicy tomato juice (V-8)
Salt to taste

SOUP: Put tomatoes, onion, garlic, lemon juice, Pace Picante, and cilantro in blender. Blend until smooth. Thin down with spicy tomato juice if mixture is too thick. Season with salt.

---

1 small zucchini, seeded and
   cut into *tiny* cubes
1 small cucumber, seeded,
   peeled and cut into *tiny* cubes
2 stalks celery, cut into *tiny*
   cubes
1 pound cooked crawfish
   pieces, body only

TO ASSEMBLE: Add raw zucchini, cucumber, and celery pieces to soup base. Wash and dry crawfish and add to soup base. (It is possible to buy crawfish precooked and shelled at many high quality supermarkets.) To make the presentation effective you must buy some whole crawfish for decoration. These can also be purchased precooked. If raw, boil them as you would shrimp. If shelling your own meat pieces, remember only the body gives meat, so you will need to buy several pounds of crawfish. Refrigerate until ready to use. Adjust seasoning.

---

6 whole crawfish
18 tablespoons frozen
   guacamole, defrosted

TO SERVE: Put cold soup into individual wide-rimmed bowls. Mentally divide soup into quarters. Arrange one spoonful of guacamole in three places on rim, and place whole crawfish coming out of soup onto rim, in fourth spot. See photo on page 119.

NOTES: If you cannot find crawfish, use shrimp, lobster or crab. However, it is the whole crawfish "sneaking" out of the soup that makes this presentation so special. If you make your own guacamole, use it, but frozen guacamole is readily available and will be fine. It is color contrast that you are hoping to achieve.

Red Bell Pepper Soup

*This is a wonderful soup on its own; however, when served in the
same bowl as watercress soup, it makes a spectacular presentation.
The red bell pepper soup is low fat, while the watercress is not.
If you have some guests on restricted diets, they can be offered
only the red bell pepper soup.*

1/2 cup chicken broth
1/2 cup chopped onion
3 cloves garlic, chopped
2 cans chicken broth
3 red bell peppers, roasted
   and peeled
1 teaspoon dried thyme
Salt and pepper

RED PEPPER SOUP: Put 1/2 cup chicken broth in 3-quart
sauté pan. Add onion and garlic. Sauté until vegetables
are soft. Add 2 additional cans of broth, red bell peppers
and thyme. Cook for 15 minutes to infuse flavor of red
bell peppers and thyme into broth. Cool. Purée in blender.
Season with salt and pepper. If soup is too thick, thin
down with additional broth.

Fresh thyme leaves

TO SERVE: Reheat before serving. Garnish with fresh thyme
leaves. If serving with Watercress Soup, ladle both soups
into one bowl. There is no trick. They will stay separate.

Watercress Soup

SERVES 4-6

2 bunches watercress
4 tablespoons butter
1/2 cup chopped green onion
1 cup chopped leek
1/2 cup chopped celery
4 tablespoons flour
2 cups chicken broth
1/2 cup heavy cream
Reserved, blanched watercress
Salt and pepper

WATERCRESS SOUP: Wash watercress. Remove all large stems. Bring small pot of water to boil. Blanch watercress for 5 seconds. Drain. Squeeze out all moisture. This will keep watercress green. Melt butter in 3-quart sauté pan. Add green onion, leek, and celery. Sauté over moderate heat until vegetables are soft, about 5 minutes. Stir occasionally. When vegetables are soft, add flour. Cook 1-2 minutes. Add broth and cream all at once. Turn heat to high. Cook until mixture is thick, stirring constantly. If mixture is too thick, thin down with additional broth. Add watercress. Season with salt and pepper. Purée in blender.

1/2 cup sour cream
2-3 tablespoons milk

TO ASSEMBLE AND SERVE: Heat soup. Serve alone or with Red Bell Pepper soup. To garnish soup, barely thin sour cream with milk until consistency is thin enough to pour out of a plastic squeeze bottle, yet hold its shape. Put sour cream in plastic squeeze bottle and use it to make decorative designs on top of soup.

NOTE: Use this idea as a springboard for creativity. I have been served puréed white bean and black bean soup in the same bowl. It is a dramatic presentation. Any soups can be served in the same bowl, except very light soups such as consommés. The only thing to consider when creating such a dish is what colors and flavors compliment each other. Spring Soup and Carrot Soup are pictured in same bowl on page 129.

Shrimp Gumbo

SERVES 6-8

This is a hearty soup that can stand alone as a winter luncheon or dinner entrée. It is also valuable because it is low in fat and calories.

1/4 cup olive oil
1 1/2 large green bell peppers,
    chopped
1 large onion, chopped
2-3 cloves garlic, chopped
1 28-ounce can chopped
    tomatoes, undrained
2-3 cups water
1/4 cup chopped parsley
1 bay leaf
2 teaspoons thyme
1 tablespoon tomato paste
6 cups okra, cut into
    1/2-inch pieces
2 pounds raw shrimp, peeled,
    and cut into 1/2-inch pieces
Salt and Tabasco

GUMBO: Heat olive oil in 3-quart sauté pan. Add green bell pepper, onion, and garlic. Cook slowly for 20 minutes. (Slow cooking vegetables allows them to release their juices.) Add tomatoes, water, parsley, bay leaf, thyme, tomato paste, and okra. Cook 30 minutes, or until thickened and okra is tender. Add shrimp. Cook an additional five minutes, or until done. Season with salt and Tabasco to taste. Thin soup with water if necessary.

---

2 cups rice
1/2 cup chopped green onion

TO SERVE: Reheat and serve in large bowls accompanied by small bowls of rice and chopped green onion.

VARIATIONS: Make this into seafood gumbo by substituting 1 pound of crab for half the shrimp. Add raw rice to gumbo for final 30 minutes of cooking time.

Grilled Shrimp and White Bean Soup

SERVES 6-8

I was served a variation of this soup at American Place, a New York restaurant. My son bet me I could not duplicate the dish. Here is the result of my attempt to recreate a unique taste treat.

4 tablespoons butter

3 stalks celery, diced

1 large potato, peeled and diced

4 tablespoons flour

2 cups chicken broth

1 cup heavy cream

1 tablespoon tomato paste

2-3 tablespoons Great Northern
white beans, puréed
(canned beans are fine)

1 tablespoon thyme powder

2 tablespoons lemon juice

Salt and freshly ground black
pepper to taste

1/2 pound small shrimp,
peeled, with tails removed

Olive oil

SOUP: Melt butter in 3-quart sauté pan. Add celery and potato. Sauté over moderately low heat until beginning to soften, about 5-8 minutes. Add flour. Cook 1-2 minutes. Add chicken broth and cream all at once. Turn heat to high. Whisk constantly until mixture is smooth and thick. Add additional broth if soup becomes too thick. Add tomato paste and 2-3 tablespoons puréed white beans. Season with thyme, lemon juice, salt and freshly ground black pepper. Continue to cook soup over moderately low heat until vegetables are tender. Peel shrimp. Coat grill pan with small amount of olive oil and heat. Grill shrimp over high heat until done and slightly charred. Add to soup.

Fresh chives, chopped
(1/2 teaspoon per serving)

TO SERVE: Reheat soup. Check seasoning. Top with chopped fresh chives.

Spring Soup

When I asked students to submit their favorite recipes, ones they would like to have included in my cookbook, this was not only the first recipe I received, but one of the most requested. I taught it in a 1985 Cusinart Class. It is hard to believe that I once taught classes on ways to make this invaluable machine useful. This soup requires no cooking, is easy, and truly wonderful.

1 cucumber, seeded, partially
   peeled and cubed
1-2 green onions, chopped,
   1-inch of green only
1 avocado, peeled and seeded
1 can chicken broth
1 cup sour cream, or
   plain yogurt
Juice of 2 limes
Salt and Tabasco to taste

SOUP: Place cucumber, green onion, avocado, chicken broth, sour cream, and lime juice in blender. Blend until smooth. Season with salt and Tabasco. Refrigerate.

1/4 cup diced green onion
1/2 cup diced cucumber,
   partially peeled

TO SERVE: Serve cold. Mix green onion and cucumber together and lightly sprinkle on top of soup.

Classic French Onion Soup

SERVES 4-6

French onion soup is one of my favorite dishes. What makes this recipe special is the manner in which the onions are cooked. They are cooked slowly to release their natural juices. Sugar is then added and the onions are cooked at a higher temperature allowing them to caramelize. Beef broth gives the soup a rich taste. An added attraction of this dish is that it is relatively low in fat.

---

3 tablespoons butter
2 tablespoons olive oil
5 cups thinly sliced yellow onions
   (about 3 medium onions)
1 teaspoon pepper
1 tablespoon sugar
4 tablespoons flour
2-4 cups beef broth
1/2 cup dry white wine
Salt and pepper to taste

FRENCH ONION SOUP: Melt butter and oil in a 5-quart sauté pan. Add onions. Add pepper. Do not add salt at this time. Cook onions slowly, covered, over low heat for 15 minutes. Uncover. Add sugar. Raise heat to moderately high and cook onions 30-40 minutes more, stirring often. Onions will turn a golden brown. Watch them carefully, so they do not burn. When onions are properly browned, stir in flour. Cook for 1-2 minutes, stirring, until no traces of flour appear. Add 3 cups beef broth. Turn heat to high. Cook, stirring constantly, until mixture thickens. Add white wine. Thin soup with additional broth if necessary. Season with salt and pepper.

1/2 loaf French bread
1/2 stick butter, melted

CROUTONS: Cut a small loaf of French bread into rounds. Brush each round with melted butter. Bake in a 250°F oven for one hour or until crisp and dry.

1-2 cups grated Swiss cheese
Olive oil

TO ASSEMBLE AND SERVE: Bring soup to a boil. Put into one large or several individual ovenproof dishes. Place the croutons on top. Cover with grated Swiss cheese. Drizzle with 1 tablespoon olive oil or butter. Broil several minutes until the cheese is browned and melted.

NOTES: Yellow onions make a difference. Do not substitute white onions. Sugar helps the onions caramelize. Do not add salt before onions caramelize. Soup can be frozen before adding croutons and cheese. If following a low fat diet, omit the cheese topping and use cornstarch instead of butter and flour to thicken soup.

French Vegetable Soup

SERVES 6-8

*I taught this soup in l987. At that time, since we were not concerned
with fat intake, butter was used for all sautéing. Today, however, I
often sauté vegetables in broth instead of butter to eliminate
unnecessary fat. I have used this low fat technique in this recipe.
You may further reduce the fat by buying a fat-free chicken
broth or making your own.*

1 medium leek, minus the
   dark green
1/2 cup chopped carrots
1/2 cup chopped turnip
1 cup chopped celery
2 cups chopped cabbage
2 cups peeled white potato,
   chopped
4-5 cups chicken broth
1 10-ounce can chopped
   tomatoes, drained
1 teaspoon dried sweet basil
1 teaspoon dried thyme
Salt and freshly ground
   black pepper
1/3 cup Pace Picante Sauce

SOUP: Wash leek. Slice down middle. Wash again, removing all grit. Chop. Combine with other vegetables. Cut all vegetables into 1/2 inch cubes. Put 4-5 cups broth in large saucepan. Add vegetables, tomatoes, basil, thyme, salt, and freshly ground pepper. Cook until vegetables are crisp-tender, about 15 minutes. Season with picante sauce. Adjust salt and pepper.

TO SERVE: Reheat soup. Place soup into individual bowls or one large tureen. Serve with salad and bread as light lunch or dinner. If I served it for dinner, I might consider serving some good sausage and cheese on the side. (We can't keep it too low in fat!)

VARIATION: Use any root vegetable or leftover vegetables to change taste. Vary herbs if you prefer. This soup could be unique each time it is served.

Wild Rice Soup

This soup and the following one are roux-based soups.
A roux is a mixture of equal parts butter and flour, cooked together,
and used as a thickening agent.

4 cups chicken broth
1 bay leaf
1 teaspoon thyme
6 tablespoons butter
1 cup onion, chopped
2 carrots, peeled and finely
  chopped
2 stalks celery, finely chopped
6 tablespoons flour
2 cups seasoned broth
1 cup half and half
1 6-ounce package Uncle Ben's
  Long Grain and Wild Rice
  Mix with Mushrooms
Salt and pepper

WILD RICE SOUP: Heat broth in saucepan with bay leaf and thyme for 10-15 minutes. This will enhance flavor of canned broth. Reserve. Melt butter in 3-quart sauté pan. Sauté vegetables over moderately low heat, until crisp-tender. This should take about 10-15 minutes. Add flour–this creates the roux–and cook mixture for 1-2 minutes. Be sure no traces of flour remain. Add 2 cups broth and half and half all at once. Turn heat to moderately high. Whisk until thickened, about 5 minutes. If necessary, add 2 cups remaining broth to soup to reach desired consistency. Cook rice according to instructions on package and add to soup. Season with salt and pepper.

1/3 cup tiny thyme leaves

TO SERVE: Reheat on top of stove. Serve in bowls. Garnish with a sprinkle of tiny thyme leaves.

VARIATION: To make this soup more interesting, add a variety of fresh sautéed mushrooms. I have also seen this soup baked with a puff pastry top. To do this, defrost frozen puff pastry sheets and cut out rounds slightly larger than filled individual ovenproof soup bowls. Fit rounds tightly on top of bowls. Bake in 350°F oven about 30 minutes, or until pastry is puffed and golden. It makes a knockout presentation!

Cream of Brie

SERVES 6

*The ingredients and preparation of this soup are very similar to the
Wild Rice Soup. It is the last minute additions that create entirely
different soups. Hopefully, this will inspire you to create
a new soup of your own.*

4 cups chicken broth
1 bay leaf
1 teaspoon thyme
6 tablespoons butter
1 cup chopped onion
2 carrots, peeled and finely
    chopped
2 stalks celery, finely chopped
6 tablespoons flour
2 cups seasoned broth
1 cup half and half
6 ounces Brie cheese
Salt and pepper

CREAM OF BRIE: Heat broth in saucepan with bay leaf and thyme for 10-15 minutes. This will enhance flavor of canned broth. Reserve. Melt butter in 3-quart sauté pan. Sauté vegetables over moderately low heat, until crisp-tender. This should take about 10-15 minutes. Add flour and cook mixture for 1-2 minutes. Be sure no traces of flour remain. Add 2 cups broth and half and half all at once. Turn heat to moderately high. Whisk until thickened, about 5 minutes. If necessary, add 2 cups remaining broth to soup to reach desired consistency. Add 6 ounces Brie cheese, rind removed. Heat soup until cheese melts. Do not boil or cheese will separate. Season with salt and pepper.

1/4 cup diced carrots
1/4 cup diced celery
2 tablespoons thyme

TO SERVE: Reheat on top of stove. Place in individual bowls. Combine diced carrots, celery and thyme leaves. Place small amount in center of each bowl.

NOTE: To make Wild Rice and Cream of Brie soups lower in fat, eliminate half and half and heavy creams used in thickening soups. Use chicken or vegetable broth instead. Roux will make soup thick, creams are for flavor.

Breads

Basic White Bread

MAKES 2 LOAVES

My husband's cousin gave me this recipe when I was in my mid-twenties. It became my first experience with breadmaking and I loved it. It gave me the courage to knead, mix, and form bread. I hope it will do the same for you. Few things are more fun than turning out a wonderful bread. Kneading can be true therapy, so relieve those frustrations and have fun!

1 cup milk

1 cup water

2 tablespoons butter

2 tablespoons sugar

1 teaspoon salt

1 1/4-ounce package active dry yeast

1 teaspoon salt

1/4 cup lukewarm water

5-6 cups unbleached white flour

BREAD: Scald milk, 1 cup water and butter in small saucepan. Do not boil liquids; let them bubble around edges of pan. Mixture may also be heated in measuring cup in microwave for 30-45 seconds. Put sugar and salt into large mixing bowl. Add cooled milk-water mixture. Stir to dissolve sugar. Allow to cool until slightly warm to touch. Mix yeast and additional teaspoon of salt. Dissolve in 1/4 cup lukewarm water. Allow yeast to "proof" or bubble up. When milk is only slightly warm, add yeast to milk mixture. Stir 1 cup flour into liquid. Add another cup. When dough is "pourable," pour onto floured pastry cloth. Put 2 cups flour on pastry cloth, to be incorporated into the "pourable" dough. Knead in flour and additional flour, as needed, using 5-6 cups total. Knead for 5-8 minutes or until dough becomes smooth and elastic. Spray a bowl with non-stick cooking spray. Place dough in bowl and spray non-stick cooking spray over top of dough. Cover with a tea towel and let rise 1-1 1/2 hours or until it doubles in bulk. Punch down. Take out of bowl and divide dough in half. Spray 2 loaf pans with non-stick cooking spray and place half of dough in each pan. Let rise, uncovered, for 30-40 minutes. Bake in preheated 350°F oven for 40 minutes. Tap loaf to test for doneness. Bread will sound hollow when done.

TO SERVE: Serve fresh from the oven or wrap in foil and reheat in 350°F oven.

NOTE: When dissolving yeast, most recipes call for a distinct temperature. I think this discourages breadmaking. Instead, remember the liquid in which you put the yeast must be barely warm to the touch. If liquid is too hot, it will kill the yeast and bread will not rise.

Blue Corn Muffins

MAKES 12-16 LARGE OR 48 SMALL MUFFINS

This unusual bread goes well with a Southwest menu. It is a batter bread and very easy to make. No worry about kneading. I love serving it in a basket with some regular corn bread as the two colors make an interesting presentation.

2 teaspoons vegetable oil

3 serrano peppers, seeded and minced

1/2 red bell pepper, diced

1/2 green bell pepper, diced

3 garlic cloves, minced

1 cup unbleached white flour

1 1/4 cups blue cornmeal

2 tablespoons sugar

1 tablespoon baking powder

1 teaspoon salt

Pinch of baking soda

1 cup buttermilk

6 tablespoons Crisco, melted and cooled

6 tablespoons butter, melted and cooled

2 eggs

1/4 cup cilantro, chopped

CORN MUFFINS: Preheat oven to 375°F. Heat vegetable oil in small skillet. Add serrano peppers, red and green bell peppers, and garlic. Sauté over moderate heat until softened. Let cool. Sift flour, cornmeal, sugar, baking powder, and salt together into mixing bowl. Combine baking soda and buttermilk. Melt Crisco and butter together in small saucepan. Combine dry ingredients, buttermilk, eggs, cooled fats, reserved pepper mixture, and cilantro. Combine well. Do not over mix. Butter or spray muffin tins with non-stick cooking spray. I like to use very tiny muffin tins. Pour batter in tins. Bake for 25 minutes or until tops are golden brown and toothpick inserted in center comes out clean.

TO SERVE: Serve immediately or wrap in foil. These may be frozen. Reheat in 350°F oven for 10 minutes.

NOTE: *The only trick to batter breads or ones leavened with baking powder is to mix only until dry and wet ingredients are combined. Overmixing causes baking powder to lose its ability to make dough rise.*

Brioche

MAKES 1 LOAF

I taught this recipe as part of a food processor class in the late '70s. This is the easiest brioche recipe in the world. Remember, dough made in the processor will take longer to rise. Besides using this dough as a bread, you can make two batches and use it to enclose a wheel of brie cheese.

1 1/4-ounce package of active
   dry yeast
1/3 cup sugar
1/4 cup warm water
2 1/3 cups unbleached white
   flour
1 teaspoon salt
1 1/2 sticks butter, cut up and
   very cold
3 eggs

BRIOCHE: Combine yeast and sugar. Add to warm water until yeast is completely dissolved. Allow yeast to "proof" or bubble up. This will take 3-5 minutes. Place flour and salt in large processor. Add butter, cut into tablespoons. Process on/off quickly until crumbly. Add yeast and water. Turn machine on and add eggs one at a time until well mixed. Dough will form a ball. Remove from processor and put into mixing bowl. Cover with plastic wrap and let sit in refrigerator 6 hours or overnight.

Non stick cooking spray
Egg glaze (1 egg beaten with
   1 tablespoon water)

TO FORM BRIOCHE: Preheat oven to 350°F. Tear off a large pinch of dough. Reserve for topknot. Spray a small, 6-inch brioche pan with non-stick cooking spray. Form cold brioche into a round and place in prepared pan. Make an X on the top with a sharp knife. Form the pinched off dough into a round and fit it into the X. Brush with an egg glaze. Let rise 1 1/2 -2 hours or until double in size. Bake for 45 minutes to 1 hour.

TO SERVE: Serve fresh from the oven or wrap in foil and reheat in 350°F oven.

NOTES: Double the recipe to make a large brioche. This makes a beautiful loaf and a nice gift. To enclose a wheel of brie, make two recipes. Refrigerate overnight. Roll out dough as you would pastry dough. Use a pastry cloth. Use one recipe for the bottom and one for the top. Seal with egg glaze. Bake immediately in 350°F oven. No need to let it rise. Let sit 2 hours before serving.

Cumin Bread

This is an example of a bread leavened with baking powder instead of yeast. It would be good served at a Southwest style lunch or dinner or a casual cook out. It is also a good breakfast bread, toasted and served with a Southwest style egg dish, or as a sandwich bread for an avocado and bacon sandwich.

3 cups unbleached white flour
1/4 cup sugar
2 tablespoons baking powder
4 teaspoons ground cumin
1 teaspoon cumin seed
1/2 teaspoon dry mustard
2 teaspoons salt
3 large eggs, beaten
1 1/2 cups milk
1/3 cup vegetable oil

BATTER: Stir together flour, sugar, baking powder, ground cumin, cumin seed, dry mustard, and salt. Whisk together eggs, milk, and oil. Stir egg mixture into flour mixture. Do not overmix. Pour batter into a well oiled loaf pan or one sprayed with a non-stick cooking spray. Bake in a preheated 350°F oven for 1 hour. Let bread cool 15 minutes and turn out to cool completely.

TO SERVE: Slice for sandwiches. Serve plain or toasted.

Jalapeño Hush Puppies

SERVES 6-8

My Texas roots make the inclusion of this recipe a must.

1 1/2 cup cornmeal
1 cup unbleached white flour
2 1/2 teaspoons baking powder
1 1/2 teaspoons salt
1/2 teaspoon black pepper
1/3 cup minced onion
1 egg
3 tablespoons vegetable oil
1/4 cup Pace Picante Sauce
1/4 cup chopped, pickled
  jalapeños

HUSH PUPPIES: Combine cornmeal, flour, baking powder, salt, and pepper in a mixing bowl. Add onion, egg, vegetable oil, picante, and jalapeños. Stir until just blended.

5-6 cups vegetable oil

TO SERVE: Place vegetable oil in 3-quart sauté pan. Heat until hot but not smoking. Drop heaping tablespoons of batter into oil. Fry 3 minutes or until hush puppies are browned and cooked through.

NOTE: *These can be done ahead and reheated in a slow oven but they are best done at the last minute.*

Foccacia with Pancetta and Rosemary Topping

MAKES 1 LOAF

This basic recipe offers much opportunity for creativity. Because it uses rapid rise yeast, it is quite easy. The topping can be anything, so change it each time you make foccacia.

---

3 cups unbleached white flour
1 package rapid rise yeast
1 teaspoon sugar
1 teaspoon salt
1 cup warm water
1/4 cup olive oil

DOUGH: Combine flour, yeast, sugar, and salt in mixing bowl. In a separate bowl, combine warm water and oil. Be sure water is barely warm to the touch. Make a well in center of flour mixture. Begin adding liquid. Stir with wooden spoon. As flour mixture becomes damp, take out a handful at a time and place on pastry cloth. Continue adding liquid until all flour is moist and on pastry cloth. Knead dough for 5 minutes, or until all flour is fully incorporated and dough forms smooth, tight ball. Place in mixing bowl with small amount of olive oil. Coat dough. Cover with a tea towel and let rise 35-45 minutes.

1/4 cup olive oil
1/2 cup chopped pancetta
2 cloves garlic, minced
2 tablespoons fresh rosemary
1 onion, sliced
1 red bell pepper, sliced

TOPPING: Heat olive oil in small skillet. Add pancetta, garlic, rosemary, onion, and red pepper. Sauté until tender, about 5-8 minutes.

Fresh yellow tomatoes, sliced
2 tablespoons fresh oregano
2 tablespoons fresh thyme
1-2 tablespoons olive oil

TO ASSEMBLE AND SERVE: Preheat oven to 400°F. Oil a baking sheet. Flatten out dough with your hands into a large oval or round. Place topping on flattened foccacia. Cover with yellow tomato slices. Top with oregano and thyme. Drizzle with additional olive oil. Bake for approximately 30 minutes, or until brown. Serve immediately or reheat, covered, in 400°F oven for 20 minutes. Salt before serving if desired.

VARIATION: *Possible toppings include sautéed tomatoes, mushrooms, zucchini, black beans, cilantro, etc. Be as creative as you wish.*

Millet Bread

MAKES 2 LOAVES

Before writing this book, I asked my former students to submit a list of their favorite or most used recipes. This bread recipe was sent in more than any other bread recipe. It is not only wonderful toasted as a breakfast bread, but good served with a one dish meal, such as a summer salad.

3/4 cup honey

2 cups lukewarm water

2 packages yeast

3 tablespoons vegetable oil

1 1/2 cups whole wheat flour

1 cup unbleached white flour

1 1/2 teaspoons salt

1 cup millet

1/2 cup bulgur

4-5 cups unbleached white flour, 1 cup at a time

Egg glaze (1 egg beaten with 1 tablespoon water)

BREAD: In large bowl combine honey with water and yeast. Allow yeast to bubble up, or proof, about 5 minutes. Be sure water is only warm to the touch. To yeast mixture, add oil, whole wheat flour, 1 cup white flour, and salt. Combine mixture well. Cover and let sit for 30 minutes. Mixture will become very frothy. Stir in millet and bulgur. Stir in 2 cups white flour. Put 2-3 cups additional white flour on pastry cloth. Pour dough onto floured cloth. Begin to knead in flour. Mixture will be very soft at first but become firm as you knead. Knead in as much flour as bread will take. Remember, the amount of flour will vary somewhat each time you make bread. Place kneaded dough into an oiled bowl. Cover and let rise for 1 hour or until double in size. Punch dough down and divide between two loaf pans which have been sprayed with non-stick cooking spray. Spray top of dough with non-stick cooking spray. Let rise for 1 hour or until doubled. It is not necessary to cover for this rising. Before baking, brush with egg glaze. Bake in preheated 350°F oven for 40-50 minutes or until loaves are golden and sound hollow when tapped.

NOTE: If you forget salt when making bread, throw it away. Bread must have salt to have taste.

Sausage Bread

MAKES 2 LOAVES

Last summer my husband, Jeff, and I were asked to spend the weekend with a former student and dear friend in Kerrville, Texas. She served us the most wonderful sausage bread. When I asked for the recipe, she laughed and reminded me that I had taught her the recipe in 1979. She also mentioned that she gives it as Christmas gifts. So thanks to this dear friend, here is my recipe for sausage bread.

1 pound sausage with casing
2 packages active dry yeast
1/4 cup warm water
Dash of sugar
1 cup warm milk
1/4 cup sugar
1/2 stick butter, cut into
   tablespoons
2 teaspoons salt
3 eggs
5 cups unbleached white flour

BREAD: Remove casing from sausage. In a small sauté pan or skillet, sauté sausage until cooked. Drain off grease. Set aside to cool. Dissolve yeast in warm water with dash of sugar. Allow to bubble up, about 5 minutes. Heat milk with sugar, butter, and salt. Heat until butter is melted. Allow to cool until barely warm to touch. If too hot, it will kill yeast. Combine yeast and cooled milk mixture in large mixing bowl. Add eggs to yeast-milk mixture. Add 3 cups flour by mixing it into liquid with wooden spoon. Add sausage. When stiff enough to pour, turn dough onto floured board or pastry cloth. Knead in remaining flour. This will take about 10 minutes. When kneaded sufficiently, dough will be tight and not sticky. Cover and let rise 1-11/2 hours. Punch down. Spray two loaf pans with non-stick cooking spray. Form dough into 2 loaves and put into prepared pans. Make 3 slashes on top. Let rise 30 minutes to an hour, uncovered, until doubled. Bake in preheated 350°F oven for 40 minutes.

TO SERVE: Serve immediately or reheat in foil in 350°F for 20 minutes. Bread may be frozen.

NOTE: When making bread, the amount of flour in any given recipe is only a guideline. The exact amount of flour you knead into the dough will vary according to the amount of moisture in the air or the amount of liquid used.

Swiss Cheese Bread

*This is one of my oldest recipes. It is wonderful for those who are afraid
of kneading dough. This bread only needs to be stirred and poured into
loaf pans. It is easy, delicious, and freezes well. It is also very moist.*

5 cups unbleached white flour
3 tablespoons sugar
1 1/2 tablespoons salt
2 packages active dry yeast
1 cup water
1 cup milk
2 tablespoons butter
1 1/2 cups grated Swiss cheese
1 egg

BREAD: Combine 2 cups of the flour, sugar, salt and yeast
in large mixing bowl. Heat water, milk and butter in small
saucepan. Heat to lukewarm, or barely warm to touch.
You may microwave liquids for 45 seconds. Add warm
liquid to yeast-flour mixture, a little at a time, and beat
with wooden spoon for 2 minutes by hand or with an
electric mixer. Add cheese, another 1/2 cup flour and
egg. Beat two more minutes. Stir in remaining flour. Let
dough rise covered for 1 hour or until double in bulk.
After it has risen, beat dough with wooden spoon for 30
seconds. Divide between two buttered, 1-quart soufflé
dishes or normal loaf pans. Let rise again, uncovered, for
30 minutes to 1 hour or until double. Bake in preheated
375°F oven for 40-50 minutes.

Butter
Swiss cheese, grated

TO SERVE: Before serving, slice bread, butter it, and sprinkle
with additional cheese. Preheat oven to 350°F and reheat
in foil for 20-30 minutes.

*NOTE: Use your imagination when making bread. Do not
be confined to baking in loaf pans. Bake in soufflé dishes,
charlotte molds or anything to create an interesting shape.*

Two Tone Bread

MAKES 2 LOAVES

*I included this recipe because it makes such an interesting loaf.
It should satisfy everyone because it is half basic white bread and
one-half whole wheat. It is also fun to make. You might try
braiding the two doughs. This makes a beautiful presentation.
Otherwise, bake bread in loaf pans.*

---

3 cups unbleached white flour
2 packages active dry yeast
3 cups milk
1/3 cup sugar
1/3 cup butter
2 tablespoons salt

BASIC DOUGH: Combine 3 cups white flour and yeast in large mixing bowl. Heat milk with sugar, butter, and salt. Heat until butter melts. Allow to cool until barely warm to touch. Add lukewarm milk to flour-yeast mixture. Stir about 2 minutes with wooden spoon or an electric mixer. Divide dough between two separate mixing bowls.

1/2 of basic dough
1-2 cups additional unbleached
    white flour

WHITE BREAD: Into one mixing bowl, add 1-2 cups additional white flour. Turn out onto pastry board. Knead in this remaining flour. Knead until dough is smooth and elastic, about 5-8 minutes for each kneading. Shape into ball, cover, let rise until double, about 1-1 1/2 hours.

1/2 of basic dough
3 tablespoons dark molasses
2-2 1/2 cups whole wheat flour

WHOLE WHEAT BREAD: To other half of dough, add molasses and whole wheat flour. Turn out onto pastry cloth and knead until smooth and elastic. Form into ball, cover, let rise until double, about 1-1 1/2 hours.

TO ASSEMBLE: After both doughs have risen, punch down, cover and let rest 10 minutes. Roll out half light dough and half dark, into 12x8-inch rectangles. Place light dough on bottom and dark on top. Roll up tightly forming two layered loaf. Begin rolling at short side. Place into greased or non-stick sprayed loaf pans. Spray top of loaf with non-stick spray. Let rise until double, about 45 minutes to 1 hour. Do not cover. Repeat with remaining two doughs. You may braid white and dark doughs together. If you do this, do not let dough rise a second time. After doughs have risen in loaf pans, bake immediately in preheated 375°F oven for 30-40 minutes. Bread will be nicely browned and sound hollow when tapped.

TO SERVE: Serve immediately or reheat, covered in foil, in 350°F oven for 20 minutes.

Whole Grain Bread

MAKES 1 LOAF

*At one point in my life, I spent ten fabulous days studying with
Madeleine Kamman in Annecy, France. She introduced me to this
bread. It has a great texture because of all the different grains and
seeds used to make the dough. It is easy to make, yet very unusual.*

1 package active dry yeast
1 teaspoon salt
1/4 cup warm water
2 cups unbleached white flour
1 cup whole wheat flour
1/2 cup hard winter wheat
1 tablespoon fennel seed
3/4 cup additional water
1/3 cup olive oil

BREAD: Dissolve yeast and salt in 1/4 cup warm water. Allow mixture to "bubble up" or proof. Mix white and whole wheat flour in large mixing bowl. Make a well in center. Add yeast mixture, winter wheat, and fennel seed. Add enough of remaining water to bind flour. Knead 10 minutes or until dough is smooth and elastic. Put oil in bowl. Roll bread in oil. Cover. Let rise sitting in oil until doubled, about 1-1/2 hours. When doubled, knead in olive oil. Let rest 30 minutes.

2 tablespoons olive oil
Coarse salt

TO ASSEMBLE AND SERVE: Place on baking sheet. Pat into flat oval. Brush with additional olive oil. Sprinkle coarse salt on bread. Bake in preheated 400°F oven for 30-40 minutes. Serve immediately or reheat, covered in foil, for 20 minutes.

NOTE: *Hard winter wheat is usually available at grocery stores that sell health foods and grains.*

First Courses

— Or Light Lunches —

Grilled Chicken Salad with Blue Cheese and Sundried Tomatoes 57
Red Pepper Vinaigrette with Blue Cheese

Coquille St. Jacques 59

Corn and Green Chile Tamales * 60
Easy Tomato Sauce *

Curly Endive Salad 62
Mustard Anchovy Vinaigrette

Poblanos Santa Fe 63
Sour Cream Sauce
Avocado Sauce
Tomato Pico *

Twice Baked Cheese Soufflé 65

Ricotta Ravioli with Fall Vegetables 66
Mushroom Butter Sauce

Rigatoni Stuffed with Chicken Mousse 68
Parmesan Cream Sauce

Salmon Cakes with Chile Ancho Vinaigrette 69

Scallop Cakes on Bed of Chinese Greens * 71
Ginger Soy Sauce

Seafood Sausage on Wild Greens 73
Mushroom Vinaigrette

— continued on next page —

First Courses

— continued —

Warm Shrimp and Scallop Terrine   75
Champagne Sauce

Sausage in Crust   76

* denotes a low fat dish

Grilled Chicken Salad with
Blue Cheese and Sundried Tomatoes
Red Pepper Vinaigrette with Blue Cheese

SERVES 6

I am always amazed when I am served something memorable at a benefit where there are hundreds of people. This salad was served at just such an event. I could not believe something so delicious and with such a nice presentation could be done for so many. It inspired me to try and recreate this particular dish. I do believe that the thickened soy sauce is the addition that makes this a distinctly different chicken salad.

4-6 skinless chicken breasts
Salt and pepper
1/4-1/3 cup olive oil
2 cups green beans
6-8 large new potatoes, cut into quarters
1 small head radicchio, shredded
4-6 cups mixed salad greens
1/2 red onion, sliced thin
3/4 cup walnut halves
1 1/2 cups large blue cheese chunks

CHICKEN AND VEGETABLES: Wash and dry chicken breasts. Season with salt and pepper. Lightly oil a grill pan and grill chicken breasts about 5 minutes per side. Chicken can be cooked ahead and reheated in foil in preheated 350°F oven for 10-15 minutes before assembling salad. Bring 2 small pots of water to boil. Add green beans to one pot. Cook 5 minutes. Drain and refresh under ice cold water. Add potatoes to the second pot. Cook 10-15 minutes or until just tender. Drain and set aside. Mix radicchio and any combination of salad greens in large bowl. Add green beans and new potatoes. Add onion slices, walnut halves, and blue cheese.

1/2 red bell pepper, roasted, peeled, and seeded
2 cloves garlic, chopped
2 tablespoons chopped Italian parsley
2 tablespoons blue cheese
2 tablespoons sun dried tomatoes, packed in oil
1/3 cup white vinegar
1 cup olive oil
Salt and freshly ground black pepper to taste

VINAIGRETTE: Put red pepper, garlic, parsley, blue cheese and sun dried tomatoes in food processor. Process until smooth. Add vinegar. With machine running, add oil through feed tube. Mixture will become thick. Season with salt and freshly ground black pepper.

continued on next page

1 tablespoon cornstarch
1 tablespoon cold water
1 cup soy sauce

SOY SAUCE: Dissolve cornstarch in cold water. Heat soy sauce in small saucepan. Add dissolved cornstarch to warm soy sauce and heat, stirring, until soy sauce is thick. If sauce becomes too thick, thin down with water.

TO SERVE: Toss mixed greens, vegetables, nuts, and cheese with vinaigrette. Place to one side of individual plate. Arrange chicken slices touching greens but to one side. Decoratively swirl thickened soy sauce in empty space on plate. If serving on a buffet, put everything on large platter. Toss with vinaigrette. Serve soy sauce on the side.

NOTE: *Chicken may be broiled but will not have the attractive markings that result from using a grill pan.*

Coquille St. Jacques

SERVES 8

I taught this recipe for the first time in 1977 when classic French was what cooking classes were all about. I retaught it in l996 after successfully serving it at a dinner party. Everyone thought this classic dish was a brand new idea.

1 1/2 pounds sea scallops
1/2 cup dry vermouth or
   white wine
1/4 cup chopped green onion
1/2 teaspoon salt
4 tablespoons butter
4 tablespoons flour
1 cup bottled clam juice
1 cup cream
Reserved juice from cooking
   the scallops
2 tablespoons chopped parsley
Salt and freshly ground black
   pepper

SCALLOPS: Wash scallops. Cut sea scallops into thirds horizontally. Place vermouth or white wine in a small saucepan. Add the green onion and salt. Bring to a boil. Add scallops. Reduce heat to a simmer. Cook scallops barely 2 minutes. Remove scallops to a dish. Reserve liquid. Melt butter in a small saucepan. Add flour and stir 1-2 minutes or until all traces of flour are gone and mixture is well combined. Turn heat to high. Add clam juice and cream all at once. Cook, stirring constantly with a whisk, until mixture is thick. Thin mixture with reserved cooking liquid if necessary. Add reserved scallops and parsley. Season with salt and freshly ground black pepper.

Coquille or scallop shells
1 1/2 cups grated Swiss cheese
Small pats of butter.

TO ASSEMBLE AND SERVE: Spoon mixture into scallop shells. Top generously with grated Swiss cheese and dot with pats of butter. Broil before serving until the cheese is browned and mixture is bubbling.

VARIATION: Use shrimp, lobster, or a combination instead of scallops.

NOTES: This dish is best with sea scallops rather than bay scallops. Sea scallops are more expensive but have much more flavor than bay scallops. This dish may be assembled the day before serving. Cover with plastic wrap until ready to broil and serve.

Corn and Green Chile Tamales
Easy Tomato Sauce

MAKES 15-20

*This recipe is always a hit. It is fun to serve as a first course with a
tomato sauce, but it is also a good appetizer. I particularly love this
dish because it demonstrates the magic of cooking. Masa becomes
a firm coating with no addition of eggs. It just "happens" to
become firm with steaming.*

---

2 cups fresh or frozen corn,
 defrosted
1 cup yellow cornmeal
1 stick butter, room
 temperature
1 1/2 teaspoons sugar
1 1/2 teaspoons salt
2 tablespoons milk

MASA: Place 2 cups corn in food processor. Grind until
puréed. Add cornmeal and process. Cream together butter,
sugar, salt, and milk. This is easily done if butter is room
temperature. Combine puréed corn and creamed butter
in food processor. Remove from processor and reserve.

---

1 10-ounce package frozen
 corn, defrosted
1 4 1/2-ounce can chopped
 green chiles
1 cup chopped cheddar or
Longhorn cheese

FILLING: Combine package of corn, green chiles, and cheese.
Use more cheese if you wish.

Corn husks (available in large
 supermarkets or ethnic
 grocery stores)

CORN HUSKS: Bring 6-8 cups water to a boil. Pour into
mixing bowl. Separate husks and place in a mixing bowl
full of boiling water. Soak 1 hour or until soft. Drain husks.

TAMALES: Spoon 2-3 tablespoons masa on each husk.
Spread it out so that when you put in filling and roll up
husks, puréed corn mixture or masa will cover filling.
Place 1 tablespoon of filling on top of masa. Roll up filled
husks. Fold in ends toward the center. Tie ends with
additional thin strips of corn husk or string. Set tamales
on top of steamer over boiling water. Cover and steam
1 hour. Tamales will feel firm to the touch when done.

---

continued on next page

1 28-ounce can tomatoes, undrained and roughly chopped
1/2 onion
2 cloves garlic
1/2 cup water
1 bay leaf
1 teaspoon dried thyme
1 teaspoon dried oregano
2 tablespoons chopped fresh cilantro

TOMATO SAUCE: Put tomatoes, onion, garlic, and water in blender. Blend. Place in medium saucepan with bay leaf, thyme, oregano and cilantro. Cook 30 minutes to 1 hour. This allows spices to infuse their flavor into sauce. Remove bay leaf and purée in food processor or blender to make smooth sauce. Add additional chopped cilantro for color.

Cilantro (whole leaves or minced)

TO SERVE: Gently reheat tamales in colander or steaming rack over simmering water. Place 1/3 cup tomato sauce on bottom of a plate. Place two tamales with husks removed on top of tomato sauce. If serving on a large platter, pour tomato sauce over the top of the tamales. Garnish with either whole cilantro leaves or minced cilantro.

VARIATION: Use refried beans or crab mixed with chiles and cheese for filling. Serve tamales on a bed of Red Pepper and Black Bean Sauces. (See page 141.)

Curly Endive Salad
Mustard Anchovy Vinaigrette

SERVES 4-6

*This is classic country French fare. To keep the original character of
this dish, you must use curly endive. Add red bell peppers for a
change, but no tomatoes, cucumbers, celery or other such "regular"
salad fare. This is an especially good companion for one dish meals.*

1 head curly endive
1 pound thick slab bacon
2 tablespoons reserved fat
4 cups French bread, cut in
    1-inch cubes
3 tablespoons butter
3 tablespoons olive oil

SALAD: Wash endive well. Dry. Tear or cut endive into bite
size pieces. This is easy to do with kitchen shears. Cut
bacon into cubes. Fry in heavy skillet until cooked but
not really crisp. Drain bacon on paper towels. Reserve 2
tablespoons of fat rendered in skillet. Place cubed French
bread on baking sheet. Bake in 250°F oven 1 hour or until
crisp. Place butter and olive oil in skillet with 2 tablespoons
reserved fat. Sauté croutons until nicely browned on all sides.
Add more oil and butter if necessary. You may freeze these,
so make more than you need.

1/4 cup white vinegar
2 tablespoons Dijon mustard
2 tablespoons fresh lemon
    juice
1 tablespoon anchovy paste
1 cup olive oil
Salt and freshly ground black
    pepper to taste

MUSTARD-ANCHOVY VINAIGRETTE: Put vinegar, mustard,
lemon juice, and anchovy paste in processor. Process to
blend. With machine running, add oil through feed tube.
Season with salt and freshly ground black pepper.

TO SERVE: Toss endive with bacon, croutons, and
vinaigrette. Arrange on individual plates or on a large
platter or a wooden bowl.

*VARIATION: Leave out the anchovy paste and you have a
classic mustard vinaigrette.*

*NOTES: Dressing may be prepared ahead and kept chilled.
Bring vinaigrette to room temperature before serving.
There is no substitute for homemade croutons.*

Poblanos Santa Fe
Sour Cream Sauce
Avocado Sauce
Tomato Pico

SERVES 8-10

My inspiration for this dish came from the Inn of the Anasazi Hotel Restaurant in Santa Fe, New Mexico. My husband and I ate one meal there several years ago. This dish so inspired me that I could not wait to create a version of my own. It is an exciting first course for a Southwest style seated dinner, but could also be used as a luncheon entrée. Fill the peppers the day before frying. Make both sauces one day ahead. This leaves only the last minute coating and frying to be done the day they are served.

8-10 poblano peppers

POBLANO PEPPERS: Sear poblano peppers on all sides under broiler. Let cool in tea towel. Remove skins once they are cool. If part of skin is very difficult to remove, leave it intact. Make a slit on one side of poblano pepper, leaving stem attached. Carefully cut inside seeds away from stem with knife. Set aside to cool.

---

2 skinless chicken breasts,
   boiled in water seasoned
   with salt, pepper, thyme,
   onion, and bay leaf
1/2 teaspoon cumin
1 cup grated Monterey Jack
   cheese
1/2 cup frozen corn, defrosted
1/2 4 1/2-ounce can chopped
   green chiles
1/2 red bell pepper, chopped
1/4 cup vegetable oil or
   olive oil

FILLING: Cook chicken breasts in seasoned water. Cut cooked, cooled chicken into small cubes. Transfer to mixing bowl. Add cumin, cheese, corn, and green chiles. Season with salt and pepper. Sauté red bell pepper in oil until tender. Add to chicken mixture. When cool, stuff poblano peppers with chicken mixture. Refrigerate, covered with plastic wrap, until ready to fry.

---

continued on next page

3 cups flour, seasoned with salt and pepper 4 eggs 2 cups cornmeal 2 tablespoons chili powder 6-8 cups vegetable oil	TO COAT AND FRY: Place seasoned flour in mixing bowl. Break eggs into separate mixing bowl. Lightly beat eggs several times with wire whisk. Place corn meal in another mixing bowl and season with chili powder. Dip stuffed poblano peppers in flour, then egg , then coat with corn-meal mixture. Heat 3 inches of oil in 3-quart sauté pan. Fry peppers, three at a time, until crisp, about 5-10 minutes.
1 cup sour cream 2-3 tablespoons milk Salt to taste	SOUR CREAM SAUCE: Place sour cream in small mixing bowl. Add milk. Stir until consistency is thick but pourable. Salt to taste. Place in plastic bottle that can be used to pipe out sauce.
1 avocado, peeled and seed removed 1/2 cup sour cream Juice of 1 lime 1/2-1 cup chicken broth Salt and pepper	AVOCADO SAUCE: Put avocado, sour cream, and lime juice in blender. Add broth as needed to reach consistency of a thick, yet pourable sauce. Season. Put sauce into another plastic bottle that can be used to pipe out sauce.
1 cup chopped tomato 1/3 cup chopped onion 1 serrano pepper, seeded and chopped 1/3 cup chopped cilantro Salt and pepper	TOMATO PICO: Combine tomato, onion, serrano pepper, and cilantro. Season with salt and pepper.
Prepared sour cream sauce Prepared avocado sauce Prepared tomato pico Dried corn husks	TO ASSEMBLE AND SERVE: Make crisscross design on bottom of each plate using two sauces. Put one fried poblano pepper on plate at an angle. Place two dollops of pico off center on either side. To make this presentation truly spectacular, stick two thin strips of dry tamale husk in top of each pepper. For a buffet, make crisscross design with two sauces on large serving platter. Place peppers on top. Arrange salsa decoratively around platter.

NOTE: Thin down defrosted, frozen guacamole with sour cream or broth rather than making your own avocado sauce. Place sauce in plastic squeeze bottle and use to decorate plates. See picture on page 120.

Twice Baked Cheese Soufflé

Serves 8

This is a special recipe because unlike most soufflés, it does not have to be prepared at the last minute. Assemble and bake this dish a day ahead. Reheat before serving.

---

2 tablespoons butter
2 tablespoons flour
3/4 cup milk
2 ounces Montrachet goat cheese
4 ounces Swiss cheese, grated
2 egg yolks
1 1/2 teaspoons Dijon mustard
1/2 teaspoon salt and white pepper
5 egg whites
Butter or non-stick cooking spray
Freshly grated Parmesan cheese

SOUFFLÉ: Melt butter in saucepan. Add flour and stir 1-2 minutes or until all flour is absorbed. Add milk all at once and cook, stirring constantly, until mixture is thick. Add cheeses. Add yolks one at a time. Add mustard. Season with salt and pepper. Beat egg whites until peaks form and beaten whites do not slip in bowl if it is turned upside down. Fold some of the whites into cheese mixture to lighten it. Pour this lightened cheese mixture into remaining whites and fold whites into soufflé base. Coat individual 6-ounce soufflé molds with butter or non-stick cooking spray and dust with grated Parmesan cheese. Fill molds 3/4 full with cheese mixture. Preheat oven to 400°F. Bake soufflés in center of oven about 15-20 minutes or until centers are firm and soufflés are puffed. Leave at room temperature or refrigerate when cool.

---

4 cups heavy cream
2 cups grated Swiss cheese

CHEESE SAUCE: Put cream in a 3-quart sauté pan. Turn heat to high and reduce cream by one half. This should take about 15 minutes. No need to stir. Add cheese once mixture is reduced and thick. Set aside.

TO SERVE: Unmold soufflés into individual au gratin dishes. Pour cheese sauce around soufflés and sprinkle with grated Parmesan. Bake in a preheated 400°F oven for 10-15 minutes or until cheese sauce is bubbling and soufflés have risen and are brown.

Ricotta Ravioli with Fall Vegetables
Mushroom Butter Sauce

SERVES 6-8

*A variation of this dish appeared in "W" magazine many years ago.
I teach this dish as a first course, however, it can also be used as an
accompaniment to a main course. Although I am including the
recipe for homemade cheese ravioli, there are good quality frozen
cheese ravioli on the market. Rather than shy away from this dish,
buy ready-made, frozen ravioli.*

PASTA: See recipe on page 152.

1/2 cup chopped fresh basil

1 15-ounce carton ricotta
  cheese

1 cup grated Swiss cheese

1/2 cup grated Parmesan
  cheese

3-4 cups cornmeal

FILLING FOR RAVIOLI: Put basil into food processor. Add
ricotta, Swiss, and Parmesan cheeses. Process until smooth.
Roll out pasta into long strips. Place 1 tablespoon filling
side by side along pasta strip, leaving 1 1/2-inches between
tablespoons of filling. With pastry brush, brush strip with
water, going in between each tablespoon of filling. Cover
with another plain strip of pasta same size. Press around
filling. Cut strip into individual ravioli. Put cornmeal into
baking pans with sides. As you make ravioli, toss with
cornmeal. Freeze. Once frozen, shake off excess cornmeal.
Put ravioli into baggie to keep frozen. To cook ravioli,
bring large pot of water to a simmer. Cook ravioli 2-3
minutes or until pasta is tender and filling is warm.
Check this by removing one ravioli from the water and
cutting it in half. Do not let water boil as force of water
will knock out filling.

2-3 tablespoons butter

1 red bell pepper, sliced into
  strips

2 cups green beans, sliced if
  using Kentucky Wonders,
  whole if using Harvesters

VEGETABLES: Melt butter in small skillet. Add red bell
peppers. Sauté until crisp-tender. In another small saucepan,
cook green beans until crisp-tender in rapidly boiling,
salted water for approximately 5 minutes. Refresh under
ice cold water. Add to red bell peppers to reheat.

continued on next page

2 tablespoons butter
2 cloves garlic, minced
1 8-ounce package
   mushrooms, sliced
1 1/2-ounce package dried
   morel mushrooms
2 cups beef broth

BASE FOR MUSHROOM BUTTER SAUCE: Melt 2 tablespoons butter in 3-quart sauté pan. Add garlic and mushrooms. Sauté until tender. Soak dried morels in hot water for 15-20 minutes. Drain. Leave whole. Add to garlic and mushrooms. Add beef broth. Reduce to 3 tablespoons. Reserve.

Base for mushroom butter
   sauce
1-2 sticks butter, cut into
   tablespoons
Reserved vegetables
1 cup enoki mushrooms
1/4 cup chives, chopped

TO ASSEMBLE AND SERVE: Immediately before serving, reheat reserved sauce base. Add butter, one tablespoon at a time, stirring constantly, until mixture is thick. Do not let mixture boil. Broth with mushrooms should be warm, not hot. After sauce is thick, add cooked vegetables. Add enoki mushrooms at end. Toss hot ravioli with vegetables and sauce. Top with chives. Serve on individual plates or on one large serving platter.

NOTE: *Morels give this dish a real punch. Enoki mushrooms make it unique and great looking. Unfortunately, they are often hard to find as they do not have a long shelf life. If unavailable, no substitution is necessary. Add different vegetables for variety. If cooking for a vegetarian, use vegetable broth in place of beef broth to make sauce. See picture on page 118.*

Rigatoni Stuffed with Chicken Mousse
Parmesan Cream Sauce

SERVES 10-12

The inspiration for this recipe came from an article on the City Cafe in Los Angeles years ago. It has become a favorite for many of my students. It is great for company because the entire dish can be assembled 24 hours ahead and heated before serving. Allow five rigatoni per person for a first course. If using at a large buffet, keep rigatoni hot in chafing dish.

3/4 pound large rigatoni
1/4 cup olive oil

PASTA: Cook rigatoni in large pot of boiling, salted water until tender. This should take about 12 minutes. Drain and toss with olive oil. This will keep pasta from sticking as it cools. Let pasta cool until it can be handled easily.

3/4 pound raw chicken breast, fat and skin removed
1 tablespoon fennel seed
1 egg white
1/2 teaspoon salt
1/2 teaspoon pepper
1/4 cup chopped parsley
1 1/4 cups heavy cream
Salt and freshly ground black pepper

CHICKEN MOUSSE STUFFING: Place chicken breast, cut into large cubes, fennel, and egg white in food processor. Process until smooth. Season with salt and pepper. Add parsley for color as well as taste. With machine running, slowly pour cream through feed tube into chicken mixture. Scrape down sides of bowl after each addition of 1/2 cup cream. Season. Mixture should be light and fluffy. Refrigerate until ready to use.

---

2 cups heavy cream
3/4 cup Parmesan cheese, grated
1 teaspoon salt and freshly ground black pepper

PARMESAN CREAM SAUCE: Combine cream, Parmesan cheese, salt and freshly ground black pepper in 3-quart sauté pan. Bring mixture to a boil. Remove from heat. It is not necessary to reduce this a long time as it will continue to reduce in oven.

TO ASSEMBLE AND SERVE: Preheat oven to 350°F. Fill pastry bag fitted with plain 1/4-1/2-inch tip with chicken mousse mixture. Stuff rigatoni by piping filling into pasta shells. Discard any rigatoni that have split. Put stuffed shells in an ovenproof dish or individual au gratin dishes. Cover with sauce. Top with additional Parmesan cheese if desired. Bake for 20-30 minutes or until chicken mousse is cooked through. Serve immediately.

Salmon Cakes with Chile Ancho Vinaigrette

SERVES 8

I studied with Madeleine Kamman in Annecy, France, in 1984. She was a fabulous teacher and one who definitely encouraged her students to use classic methods to create their own innovative dishes. These salmon cakes are a result of her inspiration. If using as a first course, serve them alone with red pepper sauce. As a main course, serve them on top of mixed lettuces with ancho chile remoulade.

---

2 slices Pepperidge Farm
    bread, crusts removed
1/4 cup milk
12 ounces chicken breast,
    skin and fat removed
1 teaspoon salt
1 teaspoon pepper
3/4 cup cream

CHICKEN MOUSSE: Soak bread in milk for 15 minutes. Squeeze out any excess moisture with your hands. Place chicken, cut into large cubes, into food processor with wet bread crumbs. Add salt and pepper. Process until smooth. With machine running, pour cream into mixture through feed tube. Scrape down sides of machine periodically. Set aside in mixing bowl.

---

14 ounces raw salmon, boned
    and skinned
1 teaspoon salt
1 teaspoon pepper
1 cup heavy cream

SALMON MOUSSE: Have butcher remove skin from salmon. Use tweezers to remove any small bones. Place salmon, cut into large cubes, into food processor. Season with salt and pepper. Process until mixture is smooth. With machine running, add cream through feed tube. Scrape down sides periodically. Set aside in mixing bowl.

---

2 carrots, peeled and diced
3 celery stalks, diced
1 cup water
2 tablespoons butter
Reserved chicken mousse
Reserved salmon mousse

CAKES: Finely dice carrots and celery. This can be done in a mini-food processor. Cook in water and butter until tender, about 5 minutes. Refresh under cold water. Drain well. Combine the chicken and salmon mousses well. Add vegetables. Form into patties. Refrigerate 1 hour or overnight. Patties may also be frozen. Defrost in refrigerator before coating with bread crumbs and sautéeing.

6-8 cups fresh white bread
    crumbs
6 tablespoons butter
6 tablespoons oil

TO COOK CAKES: Make bread crumbs by breaking up white bread and processing it in food processor until crumbs form. Do not dry them out. Use as is. Coat patties with fresh bread crumbs. Heat butter and oil in 5-quart sauté pan. Add patties. Sauté until browned on both sides, about 3-4 minutes per side. These may be sautéed several hours ahead. Place patties on baking sheet, reheat in preheated 350°F for 10-15 minutes.

continued on next page

69

2 dried chiles anchos
Juice of 1 lemon
1 tablespoon Dijon mustard
1/3 cup vinegar
1 cup olive oil
Salt and freshly ground
    black pepper

CHILE ANCHO VINAIGRETTE: Remove seeds and stems from chiles. Wash well. Place them in saucepan with water to cover. Bring water to a boil. Simmer chiles 5 minutes. They will soften and their flavor will be enhanced. Drain. Place drained chiles in food processor with lemon juice, mustard, and vinegar. Process until smooth. With machine running, add oil through feed tube. Mixture will become very thick. Adjust seasoning.

Fresh basil, Italian parsley
    or herb of your choice

TO ASSEMBLE AND SERVE: Spread 2-3 tablespoons chile ancho sauce onto dinner plate. Place 1 large or 2 small patties in center. Decorate with fresh herbs, such as basil or Italian parsley.

VARIATIONS: *I have served this as a luncheon entrée on top of salad greens tossed with cilantro vinaigrette. Use a plastic squeeze bottle to decoratively pour on Chile Ancho Vinaigrette. I have also served this as a first course with Red Bell Pepper Sauce. Experiment with other sauces and vinaigrettes.*

NOTE: *Any white bread can be used to make bread crumbs, even leftover hot dog buns.*

Scallop Cakes on Bed of Chinese Greens
Ginger Soy Sauce

This recipe is from one of my low fat cooking classes. One of the tricks in making scallop cakes is to use Panko crumbs, not bread crumbs. Panko crumbs are oriental bread crumbs, found in gourmet supermarkets. In keeping with the oriental theme of this dish, I have paired the scallops with vegetables that have an oriental bent. Once you are acquainted with bok choy, chinese cabbage and other such oriental vegetables, you will use them, stir fried, as a staple in your home. Bok choy and other vegetables, quickly sautéed together, make a nice vegetable dish on their own.

---

1 pound sea scallops

1/3 cup chives

2 green onions

Salt and freshly ground
   black pepper

2 cups Panko crumbs

1 egg white or equivalent
   non-fat egg substitute

2 tablespoons olive oil or
   non-fat cooking spray

SCALLOP CAKES: Rinse scallops with cold water. Dry on paper towels. Combine scallops, chives, and green onions. Place on a cutting surface and coarsely chop with a chef's knife. Season with salt and freshly ground black pepper. Add 1/4 cup Panko crumbs and egg white. Form into patties 2-inches in diameter and 1/2-inch thick. Season with salt and pepper. If you are concerned about seasoning, cook a little of scallop mixture in olive oil and taste. Put remaining Panko crumbs in a mixing bowl. Coat patties with crumbs. Refrigerate until ready to use. Spray sauté pan with non-stick cooking spray or use a few tablespoons olive oil. Fry patties until browned on each side, about 3-4 minutes per side.

1/4-1/3 cup olive oil

1 head bok choy, cut into
   1/2-inch pieces

1 pound spinach, cleaned and
   cut into 1/2-inch strips

2 cups snow peas, cut into thin
   strips with kitchen shears

1/3 cup olive oil

Chinese cabbage, optional

Salt and pepper

CHINESE GREENS: Heat olive oil in large sauté pan. Add white part of bok choy. Cook 1 minute. Add remaining vegetables. Sauté vegetables quickly. This should only take 2-3 minutes. Season with salt and pepper. Set aside and keep warm.

---

continued on next page

1/4 cup rice vinegar
1 teaspoon peeled and minced
  fresh ginger
1 tablespoon Dijon mustard
3/4 cup low sodium soy sauce
1 tablespoon cornstarch
1 tablespoon water

GINGER-SOY SAUCE: Combine vinegar, ginger, Dijon mustard, and soy sauce in small saucepan. Heat slowly. Stir until smooth. Dissolve cornstarch in cold water. Add to hot liquid. Stir until thick.

TO ASSEMBLE AND SERVE: Place warm greens on individual plates or on one large platter. Top with scallop cakes. Drizzle sauce generously over top. You can also fill a plastic squeeze bottle with sauce and pipe it decoratively on top of cakes.

VARIATION: *Add Chinese cabbage or any such vegetable to change dish. Add sautéed red bell pepper or some other fun vegetables. Be creative.*

NOTE: *It is possible to sauté scallop cakes several hours ahead and reheat in 350°F oven. Vegetables must be sautéed immediately before serving. Have everything ready but cook at the last minute. See picture on page 121.*

Seafood Sausage on Wild Greens
Mushroom Vinaigrette

SERVES 6-8

*The magic of this dish is that it appears difficult and sophisticated
to guests, yet in reality it is very easy. The sausage casing is plastic
wrap! It makes a sensational first course for a seated dinner and
is equally impressive as a luncheon entrée.*

8-10 ounces raw salmon,
skin removed

2 egg whites

1 cup heavy cream

Salt and pepper

1 cooked lobster, meat only,
roughly chopped

4 ounces raw salmon, skin
removed, roughly chopped

1/4 pound raw sea scallops,
roughly chopped

2 tablespoons butter

4 ounces morels or portabello
mushrooms, minced

1 tablespoon chopped parsley

1 teaspoon dried tarragon or
2 tablespoons fresh,
chopped tarragon

Olive oil

SAUSAGE: Chop 8-10-ounces salmon into large chunks. Place in food processor. Process to mince. Add egg whites. Continue to process until smooth. Pour in cream through feed tube. After adding half the cream, scrape sides of work bowl. Process in remaining cream. Cream should be fully incorporated. Season with salt and pepper. Remove to mixing bowl. Add lobster, the remaining 4 ounces salmon and sea scallops to salmon mixture. Melt butter in small sauté pan, add mushrooms and sauté until tender, about 3-5 minutes. Add to mixing bowl with salmon. Add parsley and tarragon.

TO ASSEMBLE: Put 2 tablespoons filling onto 6-inch piece of plastic wrap. Roll up tightly, twisting ends to make firm "sausage." Cover plastic wrap with aluminum foil. Twist ends. Refrigerate several hours or overnight. Fill 3-quart sauté pan with water sufficient to cover sausages. Bring to boil. Add sausages. Reduce heat and simmer sausages for 10 minutes or until firm to touch. Unwrap sausages. Before serving, grill in grill pan with small amount of oil. This gives them a wonderful, tasty appearance.

2 tablespoons olive oil

1 green onion, minced

1 garlic clove, minced

8 ounces portobello
mushrooms, sliced

1/3 cup vinegar

1 tablespoon Dijon mustard

1/2-1 cup olive oil

2 tablespoons chopped parsley

Salt and pepper

VINAIGRETTE: Heat olive oil in 3-quart sauté pan. Sauté green onion, garlic, and mushrooms until tender. Remove from pan. Reserve. Add to salad greens before serving. Add vinegar to hot pan. Scrape up any pieces that stick to bottom. Add mustard and olive oil, whisking constantly. Add parsley. Season with salt and pepper. If made ahead and chilled, bring to room temperature before serving.

continued on next page

1 tomato half for each plate
6 cups wild salad greens
1 cup fresh basil
1 cup fresh cilantro
1 cup radishes, sliced
1 cup small, yellow tomatoes,
   chopped in half
Vinaigrette
Grilled sausage

TO ASSEMBLE AND SERVE: Stacked creations are a popular method of presentation. To achieve this, use half a tomato as a base on which to build your dish. Place in center of plate. Toss combined mixed greens, sautéed mushrooms, basil, cilantro, radishes, and sliced, yellow tomatoes with vinaigrette. Pile them onto tomato. Tomato will give the height. Arrange sausage slices up sides of lettuces. Drizzle remaining vinaigrette around each plate. For a large buffet, put lettuces, herbs, sautéed mushrooms and radishes on a large platter. Toss with vinaigrette. Cut sausages and lay up sides or toss sliced sausage with lettuces and vinaigrette.

NOTES: *Many supermarkets will cook live lobster on the spot, so do not worry about cooking them at home. It is fun to use a combination of vinaigrettes when preparing one dish salads. Choose vinaigrettes for color as well as taste. For example, this would be equally good with Chile Ancho and Cilantro Vinaigrettes or Red Pepper and Fresh Basil Vinaigrettes. The basic vinaigrette formula is 1/3 cup vinegar, 1 tablespoon mustard, salt and pepper and 1 cup olive oil. Add herb of choice.*

Warm Shrimp and Scallop Terrine
Champagne Sauce

SERVES 10-12

This terrine is especially valuable because it is best baked the day before serving. It can be quickly assembled at the last minute. If asked to bring a first course on a weekend visit, this is one that is easily transported and assembled on site.

1 1/2 pounds sea or bay
   scallops
1 teaspoon salt
1 teaspoon pepper
2 eggs
1 1/2 cups heavy cream
1/2 pound shrimp, cooked,
   peeled and cut into pieces
Water seasoned with salt and
   pepper, celery, bay leaf,
   thyme, and piece of onion
2 tablespoons butter
1/2 red bell pepper, cubed
   small

MOUSSE: Rinse scallops. Dry with paper towels. Put scallops in food processor with salt and pepper. Purée. With machine running, add eggs one at a time. Add cream slowly. Transfer mixture to bowl. Cook shrimp in seasoned water briefly, 1-2 minutes. Cut into 1/2-inch pieces. Melt butter in small sauté pan. Add red bell pepper. Sauté 5-10 minutes over moderate heat until crisp-tender. Add shrimp and pepper to scallop mixture. Preheat oven to 250°F. Line 9x5-inch loaf pan with plastic wrap and fill with mousse. Put loaf pan in another pan with 1/2-inch of hot water (bain marie). Bake in middle of oven for 1 1/2 hours. Let mousse cool in loaf pan. When cool, refrigerate overnight.

1 cup bottled clam juice
1/2 cup champagne
3 tablespoons finely chopped
   green onions
2 cloves garlic, minced
2 cups heavy cream
2 tablespoons chopped chives
Salt and freshly ground
   black pepper

CHAMPAGNE SAUCE: Combine clam juice, champagne, green onion, and garlic in 3-quart sauté pan. Turn heat to high. Boil mixture until reduced to 1/4 cup. Add cream. Return to boil. Boil until mixture is thick or reduced by half. Add chives. Season with salt and freshly ground black pepper.

TO SERVE: Remove mousse from loaf pan. Cut terrine into 12 slices. Cut each slice diagonally into 2 triangles. Sauté in lightly oiled 3-quart sauté pan or grill pan, 1-2 minutes on each side, or until browned. Arrange on plate and serve with sauce.

VARIATION: Add sautéed scallops or shrimp to sauce.

Sausage in Crust

SERVES 4

This pork sausage is quickly assembled in the food processor. Unlike most sausage, it is extremely lean. The pastry dough is very easy to handle and has a wonderfully light texture. Serve Sausage in Crust with a good mustard and, perhaps, hot German potato salad, green salad, and bread.

1 pound lean pork, cubed
1 teaspoon salt
2 cloves garlic
1 teaspoon black pepper
1 teaspoon thyme
1/2 teaspoon fennel
1/4 teaspoon nutmeg
1/4 teaspoon sugar
1 teaspoon sweet basil
1/2 cup chopped parsley

SAUSAGE: Preheat oven to 350°F. Mix all ingredients in food processor. Roll mixture into a long log. Bake for 30 minutes. Cool.

1 1/2 cups flour
1/2 teaspoon salt
1 1/2 sticks butter, cut into
   12 tablespoons
1/2 cup sour cream
Egg glaze (1 egg, slightly
   beaten, with 1 tablespoon
   water)

PASTRY: Put flour, salt, and butter in food processor. Process until butter resembles "little peas." Add sour cream and process until dough forms a ball. Roll into a smooth ball with your hands. Using a pastry cloth, roll out dough to a size large enough to enclose sausage completely. Seal crust with egg glaze. Decorate top with leftover scraps of pastry. I usually create a vine going down length of sausage with leaves coming off it. "Glue" design on with egg glaze. Refrigerate, covered with plastic wrap, until ready to serve.

TO SERVE: Preheat oven to 350°F and bake 30 minutes until pastry is golden brown. If baked ahead, reheat in 350°F oven for 20 minutes.

Poultry

Sautéed Chicken with Calvados   78

Chicken with Prosciutto and Gorgonzola   79
Watercress Sauce

Chicken Breasts Stuffed with Ricotta and Spinach   80

Green Chicken Enchiladas *   81

Chicken Parmigiana *   82
Classic Tomato Sauce *

Chicken Roasted with Basil and Garlic   83
Basil and Garlic Sauce

French Roasted Chicken with Tarragon   84
Tarragon Cream Sauce

Stuffed Cornish Game Hens   85
Vegetable Sauce

Mexican Doves   86

Dove Topping for Pasta   87

Game Pie Using Duck, Dove, and Quail   88

Ida's Classic Roasted Turkey   89
Giblet Gravy

Turkey Roulade   91
Brandy Cream Sauce

Shepherd's Pie with Ground Turkey *   92

denotes a low fat dish

Sautéed Chicken with Calvados

SERVES 4-6

This traditional country French dish is often requested by many of my students. I have suggested using both white and dark pieces of the chicken; to make it fancier, use boneless chicken breasts.

4 tablespoons butter
1/4 cup chopped green onion
1/2 cup chopped celery
1 tablespoon dried thyme or
  2 tablespoons fresh thyme
2-3 apples, peeled and sliced
  1/4-inch thick
3 chicken breasts and 4 thighs
2 cups flour, seasoned with
  salt and pepper
4 tablespoons butter
1/4 cup vegetable oil
Salt and pepper
1/3 cup Calvados liqueur or
  brandy
2-3 cups chicken broth
1-2 cups heavy cream
2-3 tablespoons chopped
  parsley
Salt
Pepper

CHICKEN: Melt butter in a 5-quart sauté pan. Add green onion, celery, and thyme. Sauté until tender, about 5 minutes. Add apples and sauté another 3-4 minutes. Remove to a mixing bowl. Coat chicken in flour seasoned with salt and pepper. Place 4 additional tablespoons butter and vegetable oil in same pan in which you sautéed vegetables. When pan is hot, but not smoking, add floured chicken pieces. Sauté chicken until nicely browned on both sides. This will take 3-5 minutes per side. Remove chicken to a platter. Pour Calvados or brandy into sauté pan. Turn heat to high and deglaze pan, scraping up any bits that cling to bottom of pan. Add 2-3 cups broth and heavy cream. Return sautéed vegetables and chicken to pan. Add parsley. Add salt and pepper to taste. Simmer 45 minutes to 1 hour on top of stove, or until chicken is done and sauce is thick. You may also put everything into a 3-quart baking dish and bake in preheated 350°F oven for 45 minutes to 1 hour or until chicken is cooked through. The amount of broth and cream you use is somewhat up to your discretion. You will need enough liquid to cover chicken, allowing it to simmer. The proportions of broth to cream once again will depend on your desires. The cream will make it taste wonderful and produce a thicker sauce. Vary this part of the recipe to suit your taste and diet.

Watercress or parsley sprigs

TO SERVE: Arrange chicken with sauce on a large platter. Surround with fresh watercress or parsley. Serve with buttered noodles or rice.

NOTE: Experts light the brandy or Calvados and then pour it over the chicken. For me and most home cooks, it is much safer to turn the heat off entirely, pour in the liquor, turn the heat on, and then proceed to deglaze.

Chicken with Prosciutto and Gorgonzola Watercress Sauce

SERVES 4-6

The inspiration for this dish came from an article in the Sunday New York Times. *It is a great combination of flavors.*

---

2 tablespoons butter
3 green onions, chopped
1/2 pound prosciutto
1/4 pound Gorgonzola cheese
4-6 whole chicken breasts,
    deboned and skinned
Salt and freshly ground
    black pepper
1 cup flour, seasoned with
    salt and pepper
2 tablespoons oil
2 tablespoons butter

CHICKEN: Melt butter in small saucepan. Sauté green onions in butter until soft. Remove onions to mixing bowl. Mince prosciutto in mini-food processor. Add Gorgonzola and process to combine ham and cheese. Add sautéed green onions. Wash and dry chicken breasts. Place chicken on large piece of plastic wrap. Flatten breasts with cleaver. Season both sides of the breasts with salt and freshly ground black pepper. Divide ham mixture evenly among breasts, spreading filling down center of each breast. Fold to enclose filling. It is not necessary to secure with toothpicks, but do so if you prefer. Coat breasts well with seasoned flour. Heat oil and butter in 3-quart sauté pan. Turn heat to moderately high. Begin cooking breasts seam side down. Cook breasts until brown on both sides, about 3-5 minutes per side. Transfer browned breasts to 2-quart baking dish large enough to hold them in one layer. Reserve pan in which you cooked breasts.

---

2 bunches watercress
1/2 cup dry white wine
2 tablespoons butter
3 green onions, chopped
2 cups heavy cream
Salt and freshly ground
    pepper

WATERCRESS SAUCE: Remove large stems from watercress. Rinse watercress well. Bring medium pot of water to rolling boil. Drop watercress in water for 5 seconds. Drain immediately under cold water. Squeeze out excess moisture with your hands. Chop finely. Reserve. Remove excess oil from pan in which you cooked breasts. Add wine. Turn heat to high. Deglaze pan, scraping up any bits that cling to bottom of pan. Reduce wine to 1/4 cup. Melt butter in same pan. Sauté green onion until tender. Add cream. Bring mixture to a boil. Boil until sauce is thick and cream has been reduced by half, about 5 minutes. Add reserved, minced watercress. Season with salt and pepper. Pour over chicken.

Additional watercress

TO SERVE: Bake chicken in sauce in preheated 400°F oven until done, about 45 minutes. Place chicken on platter. Pour sauce over chicken. Garnish with watercress.

Chicken Breasts Stuffed with Ricotta and Spinach

SERVES 8

*This is a great dish to do for large crowds, as it can be prepared
ahead, frozen, defrosted, and cooked the day of the party.
It is also relatively low in fat.*

2 packages frozen, chopped
   spinach
3 cloves garlic, minced
1 cup fresh basil, chopped
2 cups low fat ricotta cheese
Salt and pepper

STUFFING: Defrost spinach. Squeeze out as much moisture as possible with your hands. Combine garlic and basil in food processor. Process to mince. Add spinach and ricotta. Salt and pepper to taste. Process to combine.

8 boneless chicken breasts,
   skinned if desired
Salt and freshly ground
   black pepper
1 cup flour, seasoned with
   1 teaspoon salt and pepper
1/2 cup olive oil
1/2 cup balsamic vinegar
2 cups chicken broth
1 tablespoon cornstarch
1 tablespoon cold water

TO ASSEMBLE: Preheat oven to 350°F. Trim excess fat from chicken breasts. Place breasts between two sheets of plastic wrap. Flatten with cleaver. Season with salt and freshly ground black pepper. Spread 1-2 tablespoons of filling over each breast and roll up. Coat breasts in seasoned flour. Heat olive oil in 3-quart sauté pan. Brown breasts on both sides, about 3-5 minutes per side. Remove breasts. Place in 3-quart oven proof baking dish. Pour off excess oil from pan in which you sautéed breasts. Deglaze pan with balsamic vinegar. Bring liquid to boil. Scrape up any bits that cling to bottom of pan and reduce vinegar to 1-2 tablespoons. Add chicken broth. Bring to boil. Boil 5 minutes. Pour broth over chicken. Bake chicken for 30-45 minutes. Remove chicken to platter. Transfer broth in which you cooked chicken to saucepan. Dissolve cornstarch in cold water. Add to sauce in pan. Heat on top of stove until thick.

1 cup fresh tomato, chopped
1/4 cup chives, chopped

TO SERVE: Place chicken on serving platter. Pour sauce over chicken. Garnish with fresh tomato and chives.

NOTE: Do not substitute canned tomatoes for garnish. Fresh tomatoes make it truly beautiful. Tomatoes do not need to be peeled.

Green Enchiladas with Chicken

SERVES 8-10

Even though I love cooking with butter and cream, I realize the necessity of preparing good, low fat dishes as well. I developed this wonderful dish to meet that need.

6 chicken breasts, skinless
Bay leaf, thyme, celery, onion, salt, and pepper
1/3-1/2 cup chicken stock
1 onion, chopped
2 cloves garlic, chopped
1 28-ounce can chopped tomatoes, drained
1 4-ounce can green chiles, chopped
Salt and pepper

FILLING: Boil chicken in water seasoned with bay leaf, thyme, celery, onion, salt, and pepper. Cook until tender, about 30 minutes. Chop or shred into fine pieces. Reserve chicken and stock in separate containers. Place 1/3-1/2 cup stock in 3-quart sauté pan. Sauté onion and garlic in stock until tender. Add tomatoes. Cook over moderately high heat until most of juice has evaporated, about 30 minutes. Stir often. Add green chiles and reserved chicken. Season with salt and pepper.

24 tomatillos, peeled and washed well
1 1/2 cups chopped onion
3-4 cloves garlic, chopped
1 cup cilantro
2 serranos, seeded (optional)
1-2 cups chicken broth
Salt and pepper

SAUCE: Bring large pot of water to a boil. Add tomatillos and boil until tender. (They will lose their bright green color when tender.) This should take about 3-5 minutes. Drain and reserve. In separate small saucepan, sauté onion and garlic in 1/3 cup stock until tender, about 3-5 minutes. Put tomatillos, onion-garlic mixture, cilantro, and serranos in blender. Add 1 cup of chicken broth. Blend to make smooth sauce. Add additional broth if sauce needs to be thinned down. Season with salt and pepper.

Chicken filling
Tomatillo sauce
16-20 corn tortillas
2-3 cups low fat mozzarella cheese

TO ASSEMBLE AND SERVE: Preheat oven to 350°F. Heat corn tortillas in microwave for about 30 seconds to soften. You may also soften tortillas by heating them in hot chicken broth for 10 seconds. Drain. Fill each tortilla with large tablespoon of chicken mixture. Add one tablespoon of cheese to each tortilla. Roll up. Place filled tortillas in 3-quart ovenproof dish. Cover with tomatillo sauce. Sprinkle remaining mozzarella over top. Bake for 30 minutes or until cheese is melted and mixture is bubbling. Serve immediately.

NOTES: Herdez Salsa Verde may be substituted for tomatillo sauce if time runs short. Use 4 or 5 7-ounce cans. Spice it up with onion, cilantro, and serranos.

Chicken Parmigiana
Classic Tomato Sauce

SERVES 4-6

*This is great family fare as well as good enough for company. I have
tried it with veal scallopini but did not feel it was quite as good.
Thicker slices of chicken seem to give the dish more substance.*

---

4 chicken breasts, skinless
　and deboned
2 egg whites, lightly beaten
1/2 cup flour, seasoned with
　salt and pepper
1/2 cup Parmesan cheese,
　grated
2 tablespoons olive oil

CHICKEN: Flatten chicken breasts between two sheets of plastic wrap with meat cleaver. Place egg whites in mixing bowl. Lightly beat with whisk. Combine seasoned flour and Parmesan in mixing bowl. Dip each chicken breast egg whites, then in flour-cheese mixture. Season a skillet with as little olive oil as possible. Use non-stick cooking spray to help out in this area. Place seasoned breasts into hot skillet. Sauté until browned on each side, about 3 minutes. They do not need to be cooked completely, as they will continue to cook when finished in oven.

1/3 cup chicken broth
1 onion, chopped
2 cloves garlic, chopped
1 28-ounce can tomatoes,
　undrained
1 cup water
1 bay leaf
1 teaspoon dried oregano
1 teaspoon dried thyme

TOMATO SAUCE: Place 1/3 cup broth in 3-quart sauté pan. Add onion and garlic. Sauté over moderately low heat until vegetables are tender. Add tomatoes, roughly chopped, to sauté pan. Add water and seasonings. Cook until thick and flavors have intensified, about 30 minutes to 1 hour. Remove bay leaf. Purée mixture in processor or leave chunky.

1/3 cup additional broth
8 ounces mushrooms, sliced

TOPPING: Heat 1/3 cup broth in small saucepan. Add mushrooms. Sauté until tender.

---

1 cup mozzarella cheese,
　grated
1/2 cup Parmesan cheese,
　grated

TO ASSEMBLE AND SERVE: Preheat oven to 350°F. Place sautéed chicken in 2-quart ovenproof dish. Top with mushrooms. Cover with tomato sauce. Sprinkle cheeses generously over entire dish. Bake for 30 minutes or until chicken is hot and cheese is brown. Serve immediately.

Chicken Roasted with Basil and Garlic
Basil and Garlic Sauce

SERVES 6-8

This is one of my favorite teaching recipes as it produces great results with minimum effort. I use it quite often when teaching young marrieds or those who know nothing about the kitchen. I feel that having people to your home and offering them a dish you have prepared is a true gift. Therefore, you cannot image the pleasure I derive from having a non-cook call me and beam with pride over a successful meal. This recipe is sure to produce just those results.

---

2 large roasting chickens,
    4 pounds each
1 1/2 sticks butter
1 teaspoon salt
2-4 tablespoons freshly ground
    black pepper
4 teaspoons dried basil
2 bunches fresh basil leaves
    or 2 cups fresh basil
Salt and freshly ground
    black pepper
40 cloves garlic, unpeeled and
    baked with chicken

CHICKEN: Preheat oven to 400°F. Wash and dry chickens. Run fingers between breast skin and breast meat to loosen skin. Skin is firmly attached in middle, but do not be afraid to use force. Use small knife if necessary. Mix butter, salt, freshly ground black pepper, and dried basil together in mini-food processor. Rub half butter mixture over chickens. Place remaining butter under loosened skin. Tuck 2 bunches fresh basil leaves, stems removed, under skin. Place in large roasting pan. Generously sprinkle outside of chicken with additional salt and pepper and dried basil if desired. Roast chickens for 20 minutes. Add 40 unpeeled garlic cloves to roasting pan. Bake an additional 45 minutes to 1 hour.

---

1 cup chicken broth
Pan juices
1 additional cup fresh basil
    leaves, cut in thin slivers

BASIL AND GARLIC SAUCE: Pour pan juices with baked garlic cloves into food processor. Purée. With machine running, add 1 cup broth through feed tube. Strain purée, pressing on garlic with back of wooden spoon. Add slivered basil to sauce.

TO SERVE: A nice presentation would be to cut one chicken in kitchen. Leave the other chicken whole. Place it in center of a platter. Surround with chicken slices. Top with some sauce. Place additional sauce in gravy boat to be served at table. Whole chicken will be brown and beautiful. Decorate with fresh basil.

NOTE: *If sauce separates after sitting a while, process in food processor or blender. It will come together again.*

French Roasted Chicken with Tarragon
Tarragon Cream Sauce

SERVES 4-6

This is a simple recipe, perfect for family or a casual dinner for friends. It is similar to Roasted Chicken with Basil. The sauce, however, is quite different. At one party I served both types and found the two sauces are wonderful served together.

1 large roasting chicken,
   approximately 4 pounds
4 tablespoons butter
2 teaspoons dried tarragon
4 sprigs fresh tarragon
Salt and freshly ground
   black pepper

CHICKEN: Preheat oven to 400°F. Thoroughly wash chicken and dry it well. Mix butter and tarragon in mini-food processor. Coat outside of chicken with this mixture. Stick 4 sprigs fresh tarragon in cavity or under skin. Salt and pepper chicken on all sides. If you put tarragon under the skin, loosen the skin on the breast with your fingers. Place chicken in roasting pan and roast 1 to 1 1/2 hours.

2 tablespoons reserved
   cooking fat
1/2 cup white wine
2 tablespoons flour
2 cups half and half cream
   or 2 cups chicken broth
1/3 cup fresh tarragon leaves,
   minced

TARRAGON CREAM SAUCE: Remove chicken to platter. Pour out excess fat from roasting pan, reserving 2 tablespoons. Deglaze pan with wine, scraping up all cooked pieces that cling to bottom. Add reserved 2 tablespoons fat and 2 tablespoons flour. Cook 1-2 minutes or until all flour is absorbed and has cooked slightly. Add half and half all at once. Over high heat, whisk constantly, until mixture is thick. Add minced tarragon leaves. Amount depends on your taste. Just remember that tarragon is a strong taste, so go slowly. Thin sauce with chicken broth, if desired.

Fresh tarragon
Italian parsley

TO SERVE: Arrange chicken on a platter. Pour sauce over or serve on the side. Decorate platter with fresh tarragon or Italian parsley.

VARIATION: Add currants, green peppercorns, and thyme instead of tarragon for a holiday meal.

NOTE: You do not need to use cream. Plain chicken broth will make good gravy. A tablespoon of Glace de Poulet Gold will enhance taste and color of sauce.

Stuffed Cornish Game Hens with Vegetable Sauce

Serves 4-6

*Cornish game hens are an underated bird. I feel they receive a
bad name because they are so often served at large benefits,
where they are overcooked and served dry. If cooked properly,
these are moist, delicious birds.*

1/4 cup olive oil
1 pound Italian sausage
1/2 cup chopped green onion
4 cups mashed potatoes with
   milk and butter
Salt and pepper

STUFFING: Heat oil in 3-quart sauté pan. Add sausage and green onion. Stir often, crumbling sausage as mixture cooks. Sauté until sausage is done. Remove mixture to mixing bowl. Combine potatoes and cooked sausage. Heat until mixture is well combined. Check seasoning. Cool.

4 whole cornish game hens
Salt and freshly ground
   black pepper

HENS: Preheat oven to 400°F. Split hens open down the back from neck to tail. Remove all bones except leg bones. Season well with salt and freshly ground black pepper. Stuff hens with potato and sausage mixture. Place in roasting pan (not glass). Bake for 40-45 minutes.

4 tablespoons butter
1 carrot, finely chopped
2 celery sticks, finely chopped
1 medium onion, finely
   chopped
3 cloves garlic, chopped
4 tablespoons flour
3-4 cups of chicken broth
2 tablespoons tomato paste
Salt and pepper

VEGETABLE SAUCE: Melt butter in 3-quart sauté pan. Add carrot, celery, onion, and garlic. Sauté until tender, about 5 minutes. Add flour and cook, stirring, for 1-2 minutes. Add 3 cups broth and the tomato paste. Turn heat to high and cook, stirring occasionally, until mixture is thick. Use the extra cup of broth if you feel the sauce needs to be thinner. Season with salt and pepper. Serve as is or strain. If you strain the sauce, put it in a strainer with the vegetables and, using a wooden spoon, press on the vegetables until all the sauce has been strained into a 2 1/2 or 3-quart saucepan. Reheat before serving.

TO SERVE: Place sauce on one large platter or on individual plates. Arrange game birds on top of sauce. Decorate platter or plate with fresh herbs.

VARIATION: Cornish hens can be baked whole. Wash and dry well. Season with salt and pepper. Bake in preheated 400°F oven for 45 minutes to 1 hour. Melt 1/2 cup apricot preserves and 1/4 cup water in small saucepan. Brush hens with glaze and bake an additional 5 minutes. To serve, place on platter and garnish with watercress and orange slices.

Mexican Doves

In South Texas, dove hunting is a favorite pastime and many of my students enjoy cooking them. I created this dish to provide an alternative to traditional methods of cooking game birds. You may substitute quail or any game bird. (Chicken may be used, but it will not be as unusual.)

---

20 doves
2 cups flour, seasoned with
   salt and pepper
1/3 cup olive oil
1/3 cup tequila
6 tablespoons butter
2-3 cloves garlic, chopped
6 tablespoons flour
1 teaspoon cumin
4 cups chicken broth or
   beef broth
1/2 cup Pace Picante Sauce
1 box frozen corn, defrosted
2 tablespoons chopped
   cilantro
Salt and pepper

DOVES: Wash and dry doves. Coat doves in seasoned flour. Heat oil in large skillet or sauté pan until hot but not smoking. Add doves and cook over moderately high heat until birds are well browned. Add more oil if necessary. Once browned, remove birds to a mixing bowl. Pour out any excess oil. Add tequila and deglaze pan over high heat, scraping up all bits that cling to the bottom of pan. In the same pan, melt butter. Add garlic and sauté over low heat until garlic is tender, 1-2 minutes. Add flour and whisk together. Add cumin and cook for several minutes. Add 2 cups chicken or beef broth. Turn heat to high and whisk constantly until sauce becomes thick. Thin down sauce with remaining broth. Return birds to this pan. Add picante sauce, corn, and cilantro. Cook 1 hour over low heat or until birds are tender. Add additional stock if mixture becomes too thick. Season.

Fresh chopped cilantro
1-2 avocados, chopped

TO SERVE: Place heated birds in serving dish. Garnish top with chopped cilantro and chopped avocado. Serve with cornbread, salad, and fideo.

NOTES: Add as many birds as you want. Allow 3-4 per person. Birds are served whole, not deboned. This enables you to feed more people with fewer birds.

Dove Topping for Pasta

SERVES 6

This is one of my most requested recipes. I created it for a Southwest Class where I also demonstrated homemade jalapeño pasta. However, make it easy on yourself. Use a good store-bought pasta of your choice. Dress it up with this sauce and presentation and have a great evening!

---

12 doves
6 quail
1/2 onion, with skin
1 bay leaf
1 teaspoon each dried thyme, oregano, marjoram and parsley
Salt and pepper

GAME BIRDS: Wash birds well. Remove any remaining feathers. Place in large pot of water with onion and seasonings. Bring to boil. Boil birds until tender. Skim off any scum that rises to surface. Cooking time should be about 30 minutes. Cool birds in broth. Remove birds from broth. Remove skin and bones. Leave meat in large bite size pieces. Set aside. Reserve stock.

---

3 tablespoons olive oil
8 ounces mushrooms
1/2 cup onion, chopped
2 cloves garlic, chopped
1 14.5-ounce can chopped tomatoes, drained
2 tablespoons cilantro
4 tablespoons butter
4 tablespoons flour
2-4 cups reserved stock
1/2 cup heavy cream (optional)
Salt and pepper
1 tablespoon Bovril or demi-glace

TOPPING: Heat olive oil in 3-quart sauté pan. Add mushrooms, onion and garlic. Sauté until vegetables are soft, about 5 minutes. Add tomatoes. Sauté 1-2 minutes. Add cilantro. Remove mixture from pan. Reserve. Add butter to same pan. When melted, add 4 tablespoons flour. Cook, stirring, until all traces of flour are gone, about 1-2 minutes. Add 2 cups reserved stock and cream all at once. Turn heat to high. Continue cooking, stirring constantly, until thickened. If necessary, add additional stock to thin sauce. Add pieces of game meat and sautéed vegetables. Season with salt and pepper. Add Bovril or demi-glace to give sauce an extra punch.

---

1 pound fettuccine, cooked al dente
Fresh asparagus, cooked crisp
Canned black beans, washed
Thin, toasted tortilla strips

TO SERVE: Heat topping. Add to cooked, drained pasta of your choice. To serve formally, plate this dish in kitchen. Place small amount of cooked pasta in center of plate. Top with sauce. Arrange 4 asparagus spears at quarter angles on plate extending from center pasta. Place a spoonful of black beans in between asparagus spears. Top with toasted tortilla strips. To serve for a crowd, place pasta on large platter. Top with sauce and toasted tortilla strips.

VARIATION: Use any game birds or substitute chicken or duck.

NOTE: Cut tortillas into thin, 1/4-inch strips. Fry as you would in recipe for homemade tortillas chips.

Game Pie Using Duck, Dove and Quail

SERVES 8-10

This old family recipe was introduced to me by my mother-in-law, Betty Moorman. It is a treasure. It can be made with any combination of game birds or with a combination of game birds and chicken. It is nice to have a combination of white and dark meats. Recipe freezes very well, so double it and save some for another occasion.

1 duck
12 doves
12 quail
Water seasoned with celery, parsley, onion, marjoram, oregano, thyme, salt, pepper
6 tablespoons butter
16 ounces mushrooms, sliced
6 tablespoons flour
4-5 cups reserved cooking stock
1 tablespoon Bovril or demi-glace
Salt and pepper

GAME BIRDS: Wash birds. Boil birds in seasoned water until very tender, about 40 minutes. Allow birds to cool in stock. When cool, remove skin and bones and cut meat into bite size pieces. Reserve cooking liquid as stock. Melt butter in 3-quart sauté pan. Add mushrooms. Sauté over moderate heat until cooked. Add flour. Stir 1-2 minutes or until no traces of flour remain and mixture has cooked a short while. Turn heat to high. Add 3 cups stock all at once. Whisk constantly until mixture is very thick. Use additional cup of stock to thin mixture if necessary. Add Bovril, salt, and pepper to taste. To this sauce add reserved game meat. Place mixture in heatproof baking dish. Allow to cool before adding pastry top.

Pillsbury pie shells or home-made pastry (see page 3)
Egg glaze, (1 egg beaten with 1 tablespoon water)

TO ASSEMBLE: Preheat oven to 400°F. Cover cooled game mixture with pastry top. Paint with egg glaze. Decorate as you wish with pastry rose, pastry leaves, or leave plain. Cut several slits for steam to escape. Bake for 30-40 minutes.

TO SERVE: Serve immediately. Good served with wild rice or a wild and white rice mixture and green salad.

VARIATION: *To make chicken and leek pie, use chicken boiled in seasoned water–dark and white meat. Sauté one bunch chopped leeks with mushrooms. Make gravy in same manner as original recipe. Top with pastry crust. Use your imagination. Make it a country pie by adding boiled vegetables and boiled chicken pieces.*

NOTES: *Before freezing, put pastry on top of filling. This keeps ice from forming on filling which will cause sauce to thin down when baked. For the photograph on page 126, I baked this pie in small, individual skillets. Changing containers can enhance presentation and allows for lots of creativity.*

Ida's Classic Roasted Turkey
Giblet Gravy

*I credit my grandmother, Ida, with my original exposure to cooking.
She was a natural country cook who specialized in pan fried steak,
cream gravy, greens, fresh black eyed peas, pies and, to a small child,
all things wonderful. I still have the letter Ida wrote me about how
to cook a turkey. I am sharing Ida's turkey recipe because more
people than you can imagine are afraid of cooking this
Thanksgiving bird. I hope this will remove all the mystique.
Basically, oil it, salt and pepper it, and put it in the oven.*

1 20-pound turkey
Vegetable oil
Salt and freshly ground
   black pepper
1/2 stick butter (optional)

TURKEY: Preheat oven to 450°F. Wash and dry turkey. I would suggest a fresh, unfrozen bird that has not been injected with preservatives. If you buy a frozen bird, allow time for it to thaw out. It takes 1-2 days for a 20 pound bird to defrost. Be sure to remove everything from the large cavity, as well as giblets, neck, etc., which are found in cavity behind the neck. Pick skin up around neck area. Take out bagged innards. Save for giblet gravy. Coat turkey with vegetable oil. Season well with salt and freshly ground black pepper. Put butter in cavity. Put turkey in preheated 450°F oven. Immediately turn oven down to 300°F. Cook turkey 15 minutes per pound. Cover with foil if it gets too brown while baking.

1 turkey neck
1 giblet
1 heart
1 liver (optional)
6 cups water
1 bay leaf
1 stalk of celery, cut into 3 pieces
1/2 small onion, cut into 3 pieces
1 teaspoon dried thyme
Salt and pepper

STOCK: Cook innards in water seasoned with bay leaf, celery, onion, thyme, salt and pepper, at least 30 minutes. Use this as your stock.

continued on next page

1/2 cup white wine
4 tablespoons butter
4 tablespoons flour
3-4 cup stock in which you
    cooked innards
Salt and pepper
2 hard boiled eggs, chopped
1-2 tablespoons of cornbread
    dressing

GIBLET GRAVY: Remove turkey to serving platter. Pour out excess grease. (If your cholesterol can take it, add some grease to your dressing.) Deglaze pan with white wine. Any country cook would use plain water, but either is acceptable. Scrape up all wonderful bits from bottom of pan. Add butter and melt. Add flour. Cook 1-2 minutes. Be sure no traces of flour remain in pan. Turn heat to high. Add 2 cups stock all at once. Whisk gravy until it is smooth and thick. Add additional stock to reach desired consistency. Season with salt and pepper. Cut up giblets and heart. Add to gravy. Add hard boiled eggs and Ida's secret—a big tablespoon or two of cornbread dressing.

Herbs of your choice
Fresh cranberries
Other seasonal small, fresh
    fruit or nuts

TO SERVE: Transfer turkey to large platter. Decorate with herbs of your choice, fresh cranberries or other seasonal fruits, berries or nuts. Pass gravy on the side.

Note: Ida would cook her turkey the day before serving and reheat it in a slow 250°F oven for one hour.

Turkey Roulade
Brandy Cream Gravy

SERVES 6-8

This is a great recipe for those who do not need to cook a large turkey for the holidays. Several of my students have made this their annual Thanksgiving meal.

---

1 6-pound turkey breast, without ribs
2 cloves garlic, chopped
1 tablespoon fresh rosemary
1 teaspoon dried thyme
1 teaspoon salt and freshly ground black pepper

TURKEY: Open up breast and lay flat. If you need to spread it out some, use a knife to cut it open. This is called "butterflying." Combine garlic, rosemary, thyme, salt and freshly ground black pepper. Rub thoroughly over turkey. Place seasoned turkey breast in ovenproof dish. Cover with plastic wrap. Refrigerate 2 hours or overnight.

---

1 pound pork sausage
1-2 tablespoons oil
1 cup onion, chopped
1 cup celery, chopped
2-3 cloves garlic, minced
1 green onion, minced
1 6-ounce package yellow cornbread mix, or 2 cups prepared cornbread
1 cup chicken broth

Pepper
1 cup chicken broth

STUFFING: Place sausage in 3-quart sauté pan. Sauté in 1-2 tablespoons oil until brown. Remove to mixing bowl. Drain off all but 2 tablespoons of fat. In same pan sauté onion, celery, garlic, and green onion in additional tablespoon of oil until crisp-tender, about 5 minutes. Place in mixing bowl with sausage. Reserve pan for gravy. Crumble baked corn bread. Add 1 cup broth or enough to make a moist, but not "wet" stuffing.

TO ASSEMBLE AND BAKE: Preheat oven to 400°F. Spread filling on open turkey breast. Roll up breast. Tie in several places with kitchen string. Pepper well. Bake breast 1 hour. Add 1 cup broth to pan. Continue to bake for 30 minutes.

1/4-1/3 cup brandy
2 cups heavy cream
1 tablespoon Glace de Poulet Gold or demi-glace
Salt and pepper
Stock and juices remaining in pan with cooked turkey

GRAVY: Deglaze pan in which you cooked sausage and vegetables with brandy. Scrape up all bits that cling to bottom. Add heavy cream. Reduce over high heat until cream is reduced by half or until mixture is thick. Add demi-glace. Season with salt and pepper. Remove turkey roulade to serving platter. Scrape up all bits that cling to bottom of roasting pan. If necessary, add additional broth. Reduce to 1 cup. Add to cream mixture. Add any reserved stuffing to gravy.

TO SERVE: Let roulade stand briefly. Slice and arrange decoratively on platter. Pour gravy over slices. Garnish with herbs of choice.

Shepherd's Pie with Ground Turkey

SERVES 4-6

This is a good recipe at any time, but for some reason I like it best in winter.

1/2 cup chicken broth
2 garlic cloves, chopped
1 1/2 cups chopped onion
1 cup chopped red bell pepper
1 cup chopped green bell
    pepper
1/2 cup chopped celery
2 pounds ground turkey
Salt and pepper
2 teaspoons fresh oregano
1 package frozen corn,
    defrosted
1 15-ounce can tomatoes,
    with juice
1 tablespoon Bovril
2 tablespoons cornstarch
2 tablespoons cold water

SHEPHERD'S PIE: Add broth to 3-quart sauté pan. (You may use a small amount of oil, but if you want the recipe to be fat free, use the chicken broth.) Add garlic, onion, red and green bell pepper, celery, and turkey. Sauté until the vegetables are crisp-tender and turkey is cooked. Season with salt, pepper, and oregano. Add corn. Coarsely chop tomatoes. Add chopped tomatoes and juices from the can to turkey mixture. Add Bovril. Dissolve cornstarch in cold water. Add to turkey mixture. Heat until mixture is thick. Do not return mixture to a boil or cornstarch will lose its ability to thicken.

---

4 cups mashed potatoes, made
    with low fat milk, no butter

TO ASSEMBLE AND SERVE: Preheat oven to 350°F. Fill casserole with turkey mixture. Fill a large pastry bag fitted with a large rosette tip with potatoes and pipe potatoes on top of casserole in decorative fashion. Bake until hot and potatoes are lightly browned.

Meat Entrées

Beef Bourguignon   95

Tenderloin of Beef   96
Green Peppercorn Sauce

Marinated Beef Tenderloin   97
Easy Madeira Sauce *

Perfect Roast Beef   98
Traditional Gravy

Steak au Poivre   99
Au Poivre Sauce

Lamb Chops Cajun Style   100
Jalapeño Blue Cheese Sauce
Jezebel Sauce

Lamb Racks with Mustard and Rosemary   101
Au Jus Sauce with Fresh Rosemary *

Herb Crusted Crown or Loin of Lamb   102
Fresh Mint Sauce

Crown of Pork   104
Port Wine Sauce with Fresh Thyme

Stuffed Pork Loin   105
Mushroom Sauce

Pork Loin *   106
Marsala Wine Sauce

— continued on next page —

Meat Entrées

— continued —

Pork Loin   107
Bourbon Sauce

Pork Tenders   108
Mustard Cream Sauce

Pork Tenderloin with Sesame Seeds *   109
Red Wine Sauce with Ginger *

Veal Chop *   110
Cream of Red Pepper Sauce

Veal Scallopini with Peppers and Mushrooms *   111

Veal Medallions   112
Mexican Cream Sauce

Osso Bucco   113

Venison Racks *   114
Dried Cherry Sauce *

denotes a low fat dish

Beef Bourguignon

SERVES 4-6

This classic recipe was featured in the first class I ever taught in May 1977 at the Southwest Craft Center in San Antonio. It is a dish that is truly timeless. I revised it from a James Beard recipe. Everyone loved it, which encouraged me to continue a career that has lasted twenty years. Serve it as a one-dish meal with a big salad and some wonderful bread.

---

2 1/2 pounds beef tenderloin, cut into 2-inch cubes
4 tablespoons butter
3 slices salt pork cut 1/2-inch thick
1/3 cup flour, seasoned with 1 teaspoon salt and pepper
1/3 cup olive oil
2 cups red wine
2 cups beef broth
2 carrots, peeled and cut into 1/2-inch slices
1 large onion, cut into 1/2-inch cubes
1 large potato, cut into 1/2-inch cubes
2 garlic cloves, minced
1 tablespoon dried thyme
1 bay leaf

BEEF BOURGUIGNON: Wash meat. Cut into 2-inch cubes. Dry beef pieces well on paper towels. Melt butter in 5-quart sauté pan. Add salt pork. Brown salt pork over moderately high heat until crisp. Remove from sauté pan. Drain on paper towels and reserve. Place seasoned flour in mixing bowl. Coat meat lightly with flour. Place olive oil in same sauté pan in which you browned salt pork. Add meat, coated with flour. Brown meat on all sides over moderately high heat. This will take 3-5 minutes. Add additional olive oil if meat begins to stick. Remove meat to mixing bowl and reserve. Pour out excess oil in sauté pan. Add any remaining flour from original 1/3 cup flour to oil remaining in pan. Stir well 1-2 minutes. Deglaze pan with 1 cup red wine. Return beef to pan. Add beef broth, remaining 1 cup red wine, carrots, onions, potatoes, garlic, thyme, and bay leaf. Bring mixture to boil, then reduce heat to simmer. Simmer bourguignon until beef and vegetables are tender, about 45 minutes. Season with salt and pepper.

Reserved salt pork
1/4 cup chopped parsley

TO SERVE: Put in large serving dish. Top with crunchy salt pork. Sprinkle with parsley. Serve with buttered noodles.

VARIATIONS: Mushrooms would be a welcome addition. Simply sauté 8-ounces mushrooms in 1 tablespoon butter and add to dish as it is cooking. To make dish very modern and dress it up, use wild mushrooms. Also consider little pearl onions instead of regular onions. Pancetta is a wonderful, flavorful alternative to salt pork.

NOTE: This dish is usually made with less expensive cuts of beef, but using tenderloin insures tenderness and makes it very nice for company.

Tenderloin of Beef
Green Peppercorn Sauce

SERVES 6-8

*This is a master recipe for fillet of beef or tenderloin
of beef. It produces a rare tenderloin every time.*

3 pound tenderloin of beef
Freshly ground black pepper
1/2 cup vegetable oil

TENDERLOIN: Preheat oven to 450°F. Wash meat and dry with paper towels. Sprinkle generously with freshly ground black pepper. Heat vegetable oil in 5-quart sauté pan. Brown meat well on all sides. It will take 3-5 minutes to brown each side well. Brown thoroughly on one side before turning to brown other side. Transfer meat to roasting pan. This may be done several hours before the final baking. Reserve sauté pan in which you cooked meat for making sauce. When ready to serve, cook meat for 18-20 minutes in preheated 450°F oven. Let rest 10 minutes before slicing. If you sauté meat several hours ahead, do not refrigerate. Meat should be at room temperature before baking.

1/3 cup cognac
1 1/2 cups beef broth
1 1/2 cups heavy cream
3 tablespoons green
  peppercorns
1 tablespoon lemon juice
Salt and freshly ground
  black pepper

GREEN PEPPERCORN SAUCE: Pour excess fat from skillet in which you sautéed the meat. Add cognac. Do this while skillet is hot but do not have a flame under skillet. As the brandy sizzles, use a spatula to scrape up all brown bits clinging to pan. The more brown bits, the better your sauce. Pour broth and cream into deglazed skillet. Reduce over high heat until thick, about 10-15 minutes. Add green peppercorns, lemon juice, salt, and freshly ground black pepper. Simmer several minutes. Sauce may be made ahead and reheated.

Fresh herbs

TO SERVE: Slice tenderloin. Place on serving dish. Place some sauce on top of tenderloin. Decorate with herbs of your choice. Pass additional sauce separately.

NOTE: If you are planning to use beef on a buffet table, you may do final cooking before party starts. Do not cover meat as it cools. Slice and reheat for 5-10 minutes in 350°F oven.

Marinated Beef Tenderloin
Easy Madeira Sauce

SERVES 6-8

This method of cooking tenderloin came from a dear friend,
who coaxed it out of a caterer in Mexico. You will find it easy,
wonderful and absolutely foolproof.

---

2 tablespoons garlic powder
3/4 cup white vinegar
1 cup soy sauce
1 tablespoon tomato paste

MARINADE: Combine garlic powder, vinegar, soy sauce, and tomato paste. Wash and dry tenderloin. Marinate for several hours or overnight.

---

3 pound tenderloin
1/3 cup coarsely ground
    black pepper
1 teaspoon cardamom

TENDERLOIN: Preheat oven to 400°F. Remove tenderloin from marinade. Dry. Combine black pepper and cardamom. Rub on all sides of tenderloin. Bake for 25 minutes on rack. Let sit 10 minutes before carving.

1/4 cup olive oil
8 beef ribs
Salt and freshly ground pepper
1/2 cup Madeira
3 cups beef broth
1 tablespoon cornstarch,
    dissolved in 1 tablespoon
    cold water

MADEIRA SAUCE: Heat oil in 3-quart sauté pan. Place ribs, seasoned with salt and freshly ground pepper into pan. Cover. Brown ribs in preheated 400°F oven until very dark. This will take approximately 45 minutes to an hour. Remove ribs. Deglaze sauté pan in which you browned bones with Madeira. Reduce to several tablespoons. Add beef broth. Simmer until reduced to 1 1/2 cups. Mix together cornstarch and cold water. Add cornstarch-water mixture to sauce. Heat until thickened. Do not boil once sauce is thickened.

TO SERVE: Slice meat. Place on serving platter. Pour some sauce over the top. Serve additional sauce on the side.

NOTE: If serving a large buffet, cook meat and make sauce before party begins. Slice the meat, but do not cover. Reheat 10 minutes in 350°F. oven before serving. If you prefer a natural gravy, omit cornstarch.

Perfect Roast Beef
Traditional Gravy

*Every Christmas day I serve roast beef at a seated luncheon for
24-30 people. I have tried various recipes for the "perfect" roast
beef. This method, suggested to me by a friend, is the all-time best.
The beef is cooked to perfection every time and can be done at least
4 hours before guests arrive. For this recipe, I use a large roast, but
the recipe can be adapted to any size roast, large or small.*

---

5 pound rib roast (or any size
   rib or rib eye roast beef)
1/2 cup freshly ground
cracked black pepper
3 tablespoons flour

ROAST BEEF: At least 4 hours before serving, wash and
thoroughly dry rib roast. Coat roast with pepper. Place
seasoned roast in large roasting pan. Sprinkle top of roast
with flour. Bake roast in preheated 375°F oven for 1 hour.
Turn oven off. Leave oven door shut for minimum of
2 hours.

1/2 cup white wine
6 tablespoons butter
6 tablespoons flour
4 cups water or beef broth
Salt and pepper

TRADITIONAL GRAVY: Reserve pan in which you cooked
beef. Pour out excess grease. Add 1/2 cup white wine (or
water) to pan. Place roasting pan over 2 burners. Turn heat
to high. Deglaze pan with wine, scraping up all bits that
cling to the bottom. Add butter. When melted, add flour.
Stir 1-2 minutes or until well combined and no traces of
flour appear. Add 4 cups beef broth or water all at once.
Cook over high heat, stirring constantly, until mixture is
thick. Add additional broth or water if necessary to thin
sauce. Season well with salt and pepper.

TO SERVE: Before serving, turn oven back on to 375°F
without opening oven door. Bake an additional 40 minutes.
Meat will be hot and rare. Slice and serve. Pass gravy.

*NOTES: Gravy needs lots of salt. I often buy an 8-10 pound
rib eye roast. It should feed 16-20. Cooking instructions are
the same.*

Steak au Poivre
Au Poivre Sauce

SERVES 4-6

This is one of my all time favorites and a real hit with men. The sauce is also good with beef tenderloin. It is a cream sauce, but for a special occasion, it is well worth every calorie.

4 rib eye steaks, 3/4-inch thick
1/3-1/2 cup vegetable oil
1/3-1/2 cup freshly ground
   black pepper

STEAKS: Heat oil in 3-quart sauté pan. Coat steaks heavily with freshly ground black pepper. Heat pan until just short of smoking. Lay steaks in pan. Lower heat to medium hot. Cook 4 minutes on each side. Remove steaks from pan. If cooking for company, undercook steaks, but sear them very well. Remove from pan. Continue recipe, making the au poivre sauce. Return meat to pan, and finish cooking the meat in the sauce. This will allow you to do everything ahead.

1/2 cup brandy
2 cups heavy cream
1 teaspoon Bovril or a
   demi-glace
Salt and freshly ground
   black pepper

AU POIVRE SAUCE: Pour out excess oil from sauté pan. Turn off heat. Pour brandy into sauté pan. Turn heat to high. Deglaze pan. Continue cooking, scraping up any bits that cling to bottom of pan, until brandy is reduced to a few tablespoons. Add cream. Reduce by half over high heat. When reduced by half, the cream will be thick enough to coat back of a spoon. Add Bovril or a demi-glace and season with salt and pepper.

TO SERVE: Return steaks to pan. Reheat gently before serving. Place on large platter with sauce or cut into individual, smaller portions.

NOTES: When reducing cream for a sauce, always reduce it in a wide bottomed pan. This will prevent it from boiling over. Do not be afraid of reducing cream over high heat. It will not burn. Adding Bovril to a cream reduction adds flavor and color. Bovril is a natural beef extract. If you cannot find Bovril, there are other good beef bases or demi-glaces on the market.

Lamb Chops Cajun Style
Jalapeño Blue Cheese Sauce
Jezebel Sauce

SERVES 8

The coating on these chops give them a distinctively different flavor. They are also excellent done on a charcoal grill. The Jalapeño-Blue Cheese Sauce is very rich. My partner, Sally Helland, prefers to serve these with a simple Jezebel Sauce. The flavors in the Jezebel Sauce compliment the flavor of the lamb.

---

16 lamb chops, 1-inch thick
2 tablespoons olive oil

CAJUN MIX
1 teaspoon fennel seed
1 teaspoon fresh thyme
1 teaspoon fresh oregano
1 teaspoon chile powder
3 teaspoons ground black
  pepper
1 1/2 teaspoons onion
3 teaspoons garlic powder
1 1/2 teaspoons ground cumin
1 teaspoon salt

LAMB CHOPS: Preheat oven to 350°F. Brush chops with thin coat of olive oil. Place all Cajun mix ingredients in food processor or coffee grinder and blend. Dip chops in Cajun mix, coating all sides. In hot skillet, sear chops for 1 minute per side or until slightly blackened. Remove chops from skillet and place in shallow baking pan. Bake for 20 minutes in preheated 350°F oven.

---

2 fresh jalapeños (seeded)
1 cup heavy cream
1 8-ounce carton sour cream
1/2 bunch cilantro
8 ounces blue cheese
2 tablespoons fresh lemon juice
Salt and pepper

JALAPEÑO BLUE CHEESE SAUCE: Remove seeds from jalapeños. Place jalapeños, heavy cream, sour cream, cilantro, blue cheese and lemon juice in blender. Blend until smooth. If mixture is too thick, add more heavy cream. Season with salt and pepper. Heat until warm and slightly reduced.

---

1 10-ounce jar apricot jam or
  apricot-pineapple jam
1 10-ounce jar apple jelly
1 6 1/2 ounce jar prepared
  horseradish
1 tablespoon dry mustard

JEZEBEL SAUCE: Place jellies, horseradish and dry mustard in food processor. Process until well combined. Serve at room temperature. It is not necessary to heat sauce.

TO SERVE: Serve chops with one of the sauces.

Lamb Racks with Mustard and Rosemary
Au Jus Sauce with Fresh Rosemary

I truly believe this will be one of the most used recipes in this book.
It is easy, yet impressive. Make this for your fanciest dinner party.

---

4 lamb racks (8 chops per rack)
1/3-1/2 cup olive oil
Salt and pepper
4 cloves garlic, minced
2 tablespoons rosemary
3/4 cup Dijon mustard

LAMB RACKS: Have butcher "French" lamb racks. Allow 3-4 chops per person. Trim off any excess fat. Heat olive oil in 5-quart sauté pan. Salt and pepper lamb racks. Mince garlic and rosemary in mini food processor. Coat racks with herb mixture. Brown racks on all sides. Allow to cool to room temperature. Spread mustard generously on racks. Set aside until final baking. Reserve pan in which you sautéed racks.

1/3 cup brandy
2 tablespoons butter
2 cloves garlic, minced
2 tablespoons minced fresh
  rosemary
2 cups beef broth
  (canned is fine)

AU JUS SAUCE: Pour out any excess fat from pan in which you sautéed racks. Deglaze pan with brandy, scraping up any bits that cling to bottom of pan. Add butter, garlic and rosemary. Sauté until tender. Add broth. Reduce until only 1 cup remains.

Sprigs of fresh rosemary

TO SERVE: When ready to serve, bake racks in preheated 400°F oven for 15 minutes. Allow to cool 5 minutes before cutting. Serve with Au Jus Sauce. Place racks on large serving platter. Decorate platter with lots of fresh rosemary.

NOTES: If you are having company, sauté racks before guests arrive. Do final cooking immediately before serving. To make more gravy, add more beef broth. Reduce by half and thicken with cornstarch.

Herb Crusted Crown or Loin of Lamb
Fresh Mint Sauce

SERVES 8-10

This recipe includes one sauce for two different cuts of meat. The crown of lamb is made from individual lamb racks tied together. Your butcher will do this for you. Allow two chops per person, three if you do not have many side dishes. The loin can be purchased or you can cut these yourself from the rack. I prefer to cut them myself because I am then assured of getting both the tenderloin and the loin. Two cooked loins will feed eight people. The cost of two loins will be about the same as one large crown. These are expensive cuts of meat but very easy to prepare and well worth the money.

---

1 teaspoon salt
5 cloves garlic, minced
1/3 cup parsley, minced
2 tablespoons fresh rosemary, minced
1/3 cup fresh mint, minced
1/4 cup fresh sage, minced
Fresh tarragon, oregano, thyme (optional)
2-4 tablespoons freshly ground black pepper

HERB CRUST: Process all ingredients in food processor.

---

2 lamb loins or 1 crown of lamb, approximately 18-20 chops
1/2 cup olive oil
Salt and pepper
1/2 cup Dijon mustard

CROWN OF LAMB: Have butcher create a crown of lamb for you. He will put two racks together, about 12 chops on each rack. Have the butcher "French" the racks. This means there will be no excess meat on the bone ends. Dry meat well. Coat with small amount of olive oil. Sprinkle generously with salt and freshly ground black pepper. Coat with herb crust. Fill center of crown with crushed aluminum foil. This will help rack hold its shape. Preheat oven to 450°F. Heat olive oil in large skillet until hot but not smoking. Brown only the crown or underside of the lamb. Transfer to roasting pan. Coat outside and inside of lamb with Dijon mustard. Bake for 40-45 minutes.

---

continued on next page

LAMB LOIN: Remove excess fat from meat. If using lamb loins, buy with bones intact. Cut away tenderloin and loin from bones. This is very easy to do by keeping your knife close to the bone at all times. The butcher will do this for you if you prefer. Remove all excess fat. Tie loin and the smaller tenderloin together in three places with kitchen string. Preheat oven to 450°F. Dry meat well. Coat with small amount of olive oil. Coat with herb crust. Heat olive oil in 5-quart sauté pan. Add meat. Brown loins on all sides. Remove meat from pan. Reserve pan in which you browned meat for making sauce. You may sauté meat earlier in day and bake immediately before serving. Coat loins with Dijon mustard. Bake loins in preheated 450°F oven. For rare lamb, bake loins for 12-15 minutes.

1/3 cup red wine
2 cups beef broth
1 tablespoon mint jelly
1/3 cup mint leaves, slivered
1 tablespoon cornstarch
1 tablespoon cold water

MINT SAUCE: Pour red wine into pan in which you browned lamb. Turn heat to high. Deglaze pan, scraping up all bits that cling to bottom. Add beef broth and mint jelly. Reduce over high heat for 10-15 minutes. Add mint leaves. Add cornstarch mixed with water. Over moderately high heat, heat broth until thick, stirring constantly.

TO SERVE: Do final cooking of crown or loin at last minute. Carve and serve with Mint Sauce. You may decide to serve 1 chop and 2 medallions of lamb. If you do this, do not bother to cook a crown. Cook lamb racks using same method. Browning and cooking times will be same as for loins.

NOTE: *Crown of lamb makes a stunning presentation, but the loin has less fat. Choose accordingly.*

Crown of Pork
Port Wine Sauce with Fresh Thyme

SERVES 8-10

This is a traditional recipe that seems to have been omitted from most recent cookbooks. It is a glamorous dish yet relatively simple. I taught this recipe at the very beginning of my career and it has withstood the test of time. It is still popular.

2 racks of pork, about 8 chops per rack (Have butcher "French" bones and shape two pork racks into crown of pork)
1 tablespoon salt and freshly cracked black pepper
2 teaspoons dried thyme
2 teaspoons dried sage
4 garlic cloves, minced

PORK: Preheat oven to 450°F. Mix salt, pepper, and spices together. Coat crown of pork thoroughly with spices. Be sure to coat inside of crown as well. Wrap tip of each bone with foil to prevent charring. Fill center cavity with crumbled foil. Pack it tightly into opening. This will help crown hold its shape. Place crown of pork in roasting pan. Roast in 450°F oven for 25 minutes. Reduce heat to 350°F and bake another 45 minutes to 1 hour. Remove to serving platter.

1/3 cup port wine
1 14 1/2-ounce can or 2 cups beef broth
1 tablespoon fresh thyme
1 stick butter, cut into 8 pieces

PORT WINE SAUCE: Pour out excess oil from roasting pan. Deglaze pan with port wine. Scrape up all wonderful bits that cling to bottom. Add beef broth and thyme. Reduce broth for 20-30 minutes over high heat until only 3-4 tablespoons remain. Turn heat off. Reserve. Reheat immediately before serving. Turn heat off or to very low. Add butter, 1 tablespoon at a time, until sauce is thick.

TO ASSEMBLE AND SERVE: Once cooked, let sit 15 minutes before serving. Remove foil and fill center of crown with rice, holiday dressing, or mixture of cooked vegetables.

Stuffed Pork Loin
Mushroom Sauce

SERVES 6-8

It is the seasoning of this dish that makes it so special.

1/4 cup olive oil
1/3 cup minced shallots
1/2 cup minced celery
1/2 cup minced carrots
2 cloves garlic, minced
8 ounces mushrooms, minced
1 tablespoon fresh rosemary, chopped
1/2 teaspoon dried marjoram
1/2 teaspoon dried thyme
2 tablespoons fresh sage, chopped
1/4 cup chopped parsley
1/4 cup cognac
1/2 cup heavy cream
Salt and pepper

STUFFING: Heat oil in 3-quart sauté pan. Add shallots, celery, carrots, garlic, mushrooms and spices. Cook until vegetables are tender, about 5 minutes. Add parsley, cognac and cream. Cook until mixture is thick and there is no standing liquid. Cool. Correct seasoning.

1 pork loin, approximately 3 pounds, butterflied
2 tablespoons freshly ground black pepper
1/3 cup vegetable oil

PORK: Preheat oven to 400°F. Place cooled stuffing on butterflied loin. Roll up and tie in three places with kitchen string. Coat meat with freshly cracked black pepper. Heat oil in large 5-quart sauté pan. Brown loin on all sides. Pour out excess grease and reserve pan. Place pork in baking pan and bake for 1 hour.

8-10 pork rib bones
1/4 cup cognac
2 tablespoons butter
8 ounces mushrooms, sliced
2 cups or 1 can beef broth
2 tablespoons fresh chopped sage
1 stick butter, room temperature, cut into 8 tablespoons
Salt and pepper

MUSHROOM SAUCE: Sauté bones in same skillet in which pork loin was browned. After bones are brown, remove along with excess oil. Deglaze pan with cognac. Add 2 tablespoons butter. Melt and add sliced mushrooms. Sauté until tender. Remove from pan and reserve. Add beef broth and fresh sage and reduce over high heat until 1/3 cup sauce remains. It will be very thick and glossy. Before serving, heat sauce to a simmer and add butter by tablespoons. Add mushrooms to sauce.

Fresh rosemary and sage leaves

TO SERVE: Slice pork and place on serving platter. Pour some sauce over the top. Decorate with fresh rosemary and sage.

Pork Loin
Marsala Wine Sauce

SERVES 8-10

*Pork loin is a low fat, tasty cut of meat and the Marsala Wine Sauce
is especially good. It is basically a sauce by reduction, but because of
the flour, the sauce does not need to be thickened with butter.
It can be made ahead and frozen.*

1 pork loin, approximately
    4 pounds
3 tablespoons dried sage
2 tablespoons cracked black
    pepper
1/3-1/2 cup vegetable oil

PORK LOIN: Wash and dry pork loin. Mix sage and pepper. Coat pork loin with mixture. Let sit 1 hour. Put oil in 3-quart sauté pan. Brown pork on all sides. Transfer meat to roasting pan. Bake in preheated 350°F oven for 1 hour and 15 minutes.

3 tablespoons olive oil
4-8 baby back rib bones, or
    any pork bones butcher will
    give you
2 carrots, unpeeled and cut
    into large pieces
1 large onion, unpeeled and
    chopped big
2 ribs celery, chopped big
3 large cloves garlic, chopped
1/2 cup Marsala
3 tablespoons flour
1 14-ounce can chopped
    tomatoes
1 tablespoon rosemary
1/2 cup parsley
4 cups chicken or beef broth
Salt and pepper

MARSALA WINE SAUCE: Heat oil in 3-quart sauté pan. Add pork bones. Brown over high heat, stirring occasionally. When browned, remove bones and add carrots, onion, celery and garlic. Brown vegetables over moderately high heat. This will take approximately 30 minutes. Deglaze pan with Marsala, scraping up any brown bits that cling to bottom of pan. Heat until Marsala has almost entirely evaporated. Add flour. Stir until well combined, about 1-2 minutes. Add tomatoes, rosemary, parsley, and broth. Simmer 1 hour or longer. Strain sauce, pressing solids to release juices. Season with salt and pepper.

Fresh sage leaves

TO SERVE: Slice pork. Arrange on serving platter. Top with sauce. Garnish with fresh sage leaves or with fried sage. If using fried sage, cook sage leaves for few seconds in hot oil. They will be crisp in 30 seconds. Drain.

Pork Loin
Bourbon Sauce

SERVES 6-8

Pork is one of my favorite meats. It is inexpensive yet has incredible flavor. It is amazing to me how this cut of meat can be adapted to suit so many different tastes.

1 pork loin, about 3 pounds
Salt and freshly ground
    black pepper
1/2 cup Dijon mustard
1/3 cup molasses
1/4 cup soy sauce
1/2 cup olive oil

PORK LOIN: Wash and dry pork loin. Season with salt and freshly ground black pepper. Combine mustard, molasses and soy sauce in food processor. Reserve. In a large skillet, heat olive oil to hot but not smoking. Add seasoned pork and brown well on all sides. Cool. Completely coat loin with mustard mixture. Transfer pork to roasting pan. Bake at 400°F for 40 minutes. Reserve skillet in which the loin was browned.

1/2 cup bourbon
1 can beef broth
1 stick butter, room
    temperature, cut into 8
    tablespoons

BOURBON SAUCE: Pour bourbon into skillet in which the loin was browned. Deglaze pan over high heat, scraping up all bits that cling to bottom of pan. Add beef broth and reduce mixture to 1/2 cup. Add butter by tablespoons over very low heat. You may reduce the broth long before serving, but you must add the butter immediately before serving. To do this, reheat stock to boiling. Turn off heat. Add butter by tablespoons, whisking at all times, until sauce is thick.

Italian parsley

TO SERVE: Slice loin and arrange on serving platter. Pour sauce over top. Decorate with Italian parsley.

VARIATION: Try adding a teaspoon of Dijon mustard to finished sauce.

Pork Tenders
Mustard Cream Sauce

SERVES 6

This is an old family recipe. I first taught it early in my career, but it is still a hit whenever it is served. It is not low in fat but worth a special evening. Because this cut of pork is so tender it can be cut with a fork, it is a perfect dish for a large crowd where seating may not be at tables.

---

12 medallions of pork
 tenderloin, 1-inch thick
Salt and freshly ground
 black pepper
1/3 cup flour, seasoned with
 salt and pepper
3 tablespoons butter
3 tablespoons oil

TENDERS: Lay medallions between two sheets of plastic wrap. Flatten with meat cleaver until they are 1/2-inch thick. Sprinkle with salt and pepper and dust lightly with seasoned flour. Melt butter and oil in 3-quart sauté pan. Sauté pork for 2-3 minutes on each side or until well browned. Transfer to a plate.

1/3 cup white wine
2 cups heavy cream
1/3 cup Dijon mustard
1 teaspoon Bovril or demi-glace

MUSTARD CREAM: Deglaze pan with wine. Boil this mixture, picking up all brown bits that cling to bottom of pan. Add cream. Bring to a boil. Cook over high heat until mixture is thick, about 5 minutes. Remove from heat. Swirl in Dijon mustard. Add teaspoon of Bovril or demi-glace to enhance color and flavor of sauce. Return tenders to sauce and reheat gently until pork is cooked through. Do not overcook.

1/3 cup chopped Italian parsley

TO SERVE: Place tenders in sauce on large platter. Sprinkle with chopped Italian parsley.

NOTE: Fresh herbs are so beautiful. Sprinkling dish with fresh thyme would change it slightly, but it would still be tasty and beautiful.

Pork Tenderloin with Sesame Seeds
Red Wine Sauce with Ginger

SERVES 6-8

This recipe has an oriental bent and would go well with rice or noodles and a stir-fry mixture of Chinese greens.

---

2 pork tenderloins, about
   1 pound each
1/4 cup soy sauce
2 cloves garlic, chopped
1 2-inch piece of ginger root,
   peeled and sliced thin
Salt and freshly ground
   black pepper
1/4 cup vegetable oil
1/4 cup honey
1/2 cup sesame seeds
Olive oil

TENDERLOIN: Buy two pork tenderloins. Remove any excess fat. Marinate pork, covered, in soy sauce, garlic and ginger root for 1 hour or overnight. Remove pork. Pat it dry. Season well with salt and freshly ground black pepper. Preheat oven to 400°F. Heat oil in 3-quart sauté pan. Sauté pork over moderately high heat until brown on all sides. Reserve sauté pan with drippings for making sauce. Roll pork in honey. Coat with sesame seeds. Roast for 20 minutes. Let pork stand for 5 minutes.

1/3 cup red wine
2 tablespoons butter
1/3 cup chopped green onion
1-2 tablespoons fresh ginger,
   minced
2 cups beef broth
1 tablespoon cornstarch
1 tablespoon water
1 teaspoon demi-glace
Dijon mustard (optional)
Salt and pepper

RED WINE SAUCE WITH GINGER: Pour out excess oil from pan in which you browned pork. Add red wine. Turn heat to high. Deglaze pan, scraping up all bits that cling to the bottom. Melt butter. Add onion and ginger. Sauté until tender. Add broth and reduce over high heat for 15 minutes. Dissolve cornstarch in water and add to reduced broth. Heat until thickened. Add teaspoon of demi-glace, if necessary, for additional flavor. Add Dijon mustard if desired. Season with salt and pepper.

TO SERVE: Slice pork tenderloin and serve with sauce.

NOTES: You may want to use pork loin instead of tenderloin. Loin is cheaper and will feed many more people. Directions are exactly the same except final roasting time will be 40-50 minutes instead of 20 minutes for tenderloin. When deglazing a pan, you may use any type of alcohol (Madeira, Marsala, red wine, white wine, port, brandy etc.) Sauce will vary accordingly.

Veal Chop
Cream of Red Pepper Sauce

SERVES 6

This is a simple recipe with a versatile sauce that is good on many other things, especially grilled salmon or swordfish.

6 veal chops (have butcher "French" chops)
1/4 cup olive oil
4 tablespoons butter
Juice of 1 lemon
4 drops of Worcestershire
Salt and coarsely ground black pepper

VEAL: Preheat broiler. Wash and dry veal chops. Heat olive oil, butter, lemon juice and Worcestershire in small saucepan until butter is melted. Cool. Coat chops on all sides. Season chops with salt and pepper. Broil under preheated broiler 5 minutes on each side. Or grill 5 minutes on each side in a grill pan. If you grill outside, grill 4 minutes on each side. Chops can be grilled ahead.

4 red bell peppers, roasted, peeled and seeded
1/4 cup olive oil
2 garlic cloves, chopped
1 medium onion, chopped
1-2 cups chicken broth
2 cups cream
Salt
Cayenne

RED PEPPER SAUCE: Roast red bell peppers by charring under broiler on baking sheet until brown on all sides. Cool in paper bag or tea towel. Peel and seed under running water. Put olive oil in 3-quart sauté pan. Add garlic and onion. Sauté until tender. Add peeled peppers, broth and cream. Bring to boil. Reduce liquid over high heat until thick. Purée in blender. Strain if desired. Season to taste with salt and cayenne.

LOW FAT VERSION: This is a wonderful sauce without addition of cream. I use it often for friends who are on low fat diets. Cook and purée peppers, garlic, onion with broth but omit cream. Use as much or as little stock as you need to achieve proper thickness for sauce. Do not strain. Season with salt and pepper.

TO ASSEMBLE AND SERVE: If made ahead, reheat chops, covered, in 400°F oven for 10 minutes. Serve with sauce.

VARIATION: Pork chops can be substituted for veal.

NOTE: One 14-ounce can broth is roughly equal to 2 cups.

Veal Scallopini with Peppers and Mushrooms

SERVES 4-6

This recipe is beautiful and quick. It can be cooked early in the day and reheated for guests. Serve with a simple pasta and Eggplant Stacks with Goat Cheese.

8 veal scallopini
1 cup flour seasoned with
   1 teaspoon salt and pepper
1/3 cup olive oil
1/2 cup Madeira
4 tablespoons butter
2 garlic cloves, minced
1 red bell pepper, sliced
1 yellow bell pepper, sliced
1 pound fresh, sliced button
   mushrooms
1 teaspoon dried oregano or
   2 teaspoons fresh oregano
3 tablespoons flour
2 cups beef broth
1 tablespoon demi-glace
1/3 cup chopped Italian parsley
Salt and pepper

VEAL SCALLOPINI: Dry scallopini. Put seasoned flour into mixing bowl and lightly coat scallopini with seasoned flour. Heat olive oil in 5-quart sauté pan. Sauté scallopini over high heat until brown on both sides, about 2 minutes per side. Pour out excess oil. Deglaze pan with Madeira, scraping up all brown bits from bottom of pan. Add butter and melt. Add garlic, peppers, mushrooms and oregano. Cook over moderate heat until vegetables are tender. Add 3 tablespoons flour. Stir 1-2 minutes. Add broth and demi-glace. Turn heat to high. Cook, stirring, until sauce is thick. Return veal to pan. Add parsley. Season with salt and pepper.

Fresh oregano

TO SERVE: Arrange veal with sauce on large serving plate. Sprinkle with additional parsley if desired. Decorate platter with fresh oregano.

NOTE: All meats must be dry before browning. Otherwise, they will not brown nicely.

Veal Medallions
Mexican Cream Sauce

SERVES 10

*Because veal is so low in fat, it often needs a sauce to give it flavor.
I devised this recipe for a class in Southwest cuisine using the
wonderful flavors of Mexico.*

20 veal medallions or veal
  scallopini
2-3 cups flour seasoned with
  salt and pepper
1/3 cup olive oil

VEAL: Place medallions between two sheets of plastic wrap. Pound them into thin slices with a meat cleaver. (If you are using veal scallopini this will not be necessary.) Place seasoned flour in a mixing bowl. Lightly dust veal medallions with seasoned flour. Heat olive oil in a 3-quart sauté pan. Sauté veal until brown on both sides. Once browned, remove to another dish. Add additional oil if necessary to keep medallions from sticking during cooking. Once all are browned, remove any excess oil. Reserve pan for sauce.

1/2 cup white wine
3 tablespoons butter
2 cloves garlic, chopped
1/2 onion, chopped
2 tomatoes, seeded and
  chopped
1 4-ounce can chopped
  green chilies
3 cups heavy cream
1/4 cup Pace Picante Sauce
1/4 cup chopped cilantro
Salt and pepper

MEXICAN CREAM SAUCE: Deglaze pan in which you cooked veal with white wine. Scrape up any bits that cling to bottom. Add butter and melt. Add garlic, onion, tomatoes, and green chilies. Cook 5 minutes over moderate heat until onion is soft. Add heavy cream. Turn heat to high. Reduce mixture until it is thick. This should take about 15 minutes. Strain the sauce. Add picante sauce and cilantro. Season with salt and pepper.

TO SERVE: Reheat meat in sauté pan with sauce. Place meat with sauce on a large serving platter. Sprinkle with additional chopped, fresh cilantro.

NOTES: If cooking for a casual affair, there is no need to strain the sauce. Pork may be substituted in any recipe for veal.

Osso Bucco

My husband used to rave about this dish as it was served at the old
St. Anthony Club in San Antonio. I decided to prepare it my own way.
He has never complained.

4-6 veal shanks
1 cup flour, seasoned with salt
　and pepper
1/2 cup olive oil
2 large onions, chopped
4 carrots, chopped fine
4 stalks celery, chopped fine
4 cloves garlic, chopped
4 tablespoons butter, olive oil
　(or 1/2 cup chicken broth
　for low fat version)
4 tablespoons flour (omit for
　low fat version)
1 teaspoon oregano
1 teaspoon basil
1 cup dry white wine
2 cans beef or chicken broth
1 bay leaf
1 28-ounce can chopped
　tomatoes
1-2 tablespoons tomato paste
Salt and pepper

VEAL: Wash and dry veal shanks. Lightly coat in seasoned flour. Heat oil in large, heavy 5-quart sauté pan. Add veal shanks. Sauté over moderately high heat until brown on both sides, about 5 minutes per side. Remove from pan. Add more oil if necessary. Put onions, carrots, celery and garlic in same pan. Cook over medium high heat for 4-5 minutes or until beginning to soften. Remove and reserve vegetables. Pour out excess oil. Add 4 tablespoons butter to same pan. Melt. Stir in flour. Add oregano and basil. Cook 1-2 minutes. Add wine and beef or chicken broth. Stir with whisk until mixture is smooth. (To lower fat, omit butter and flour.) Add bay leaf, tomatoes, tomato paste, veal shanks and reserved vegetables. Season with salt and pepper. Bring to boil. Reduce heat to simmer and cook 1 1/2 hours. Correct seasoning.

1/4 cup minced Italian parsley
Minced zest of 1 lemon

TO SERVE: Transfer veal to large serving dish. Sprinkle with mixture of parsley and lemon zest.

Venison Racks
Dried Cherry Sauce

Venison has recently become readily available commercially. (See page 2 for source information.) It is an expensive cut of meat but worth every cent. For best results, it should be cooked rare.

2 tablespoons olive oil
1/3 cup chopped green onion
2 large cloves garlic
2 tablespoons dried cherries, soaked in hot water 15 minutes
1 teaspoon thyme
1/4 cup olive oil
1/2 cup cider vinegar
3 whole cloves

MARINADE: Heat olive oil in 3-quart sauté pan. Add green onion and garlic. Sauté for 1-2 minutes or until onion and garlic are soft and have released their flavors. Add dried cherries, thyme, olive oil, vinegar, and cloves.

1 venison rack, about 12 chops
Salt and freshly cracked black pepper
1/3 cup olive oil

VENISON: Remove all excess sinew and fat from venison racks. Wash and dry racks. Season well with salt and freshly cracked black pepper. Place in glass dish with marinade. Cover with plastic wrap. Marinate 1 hour or overnight. Remove venison from marinade. Dry venison, reserving marinade. Season with additional cracked pepper. Brown meat on all sides over high heat, about 3-4 minutes per side. Remove meat to baking dish and reserve. Reserve pan in which you sautéed venison. Roast venison in 425°F oven immediately before serving. Roast 20 minutes for rare meat.

1/2 cup Marsala
1 cup beef broth
Reserved marinade
1 teaspoon demi-glace or beef base
1 tablespoon cornstarch
1 tablespoon cold water
Additional dried cherries
Salt and pepper

VENISON SAUCE: Deglaze reserved pan over high heat with Marsala. Scrape up all bits that cling to bottom of pan. Reduce Marsala to a few tablespoons. Add beef broth and reserved marinade. Add good demi-glace or beef base. Reduce over high heat for 15 minutes. Mix cornstarch with cold water. Add to reduced broth. Thicken over high heat. When sauce thickens, immediately turn heat to low. Never boil sauce again. Add additional dried cherries, if desired. Season.

TO SERVE: Cut cooked rack into chops. Allow 2 chops per person. Serve with sauce.

Chicken Liver Mousse en Gelée, page 15; Tiny Cheese Tarts, page 14; Scallion Crêpes with Caviar, page 23; and Venison Paté, page 26.

Ricotta Ravioli with Fall Vegetables with Mushroom Butter Sauce, page 66.

Top photo: Carrot Tarts, page 174.
Bottom photo: Crawfish Gazpacho, page 33.

Poblanos Santa Fe, Avocado Sauce, Sour Cream Sauce, Tomato Pico, page 63.

Scallop Cakes on Bed of Chinese Greens, page 71.

Wild Mushrooms in Puff Pastry Boxes, page 192.

Chicken Roasted with Basil and Garlic, page 83.

Seared Salmon with Red Pepper and Black Bean Sauces, page 141.

Seafood Sausage on Wild Greens, page 73.

Game Pie, page 88.

Venison Racks with Dried Cherry Sauce, page 114.

Succotash of Lima Beans, Corn, and Tomatoes, page 187.

Top photo: Spring Soup, page 38, and Carrot Soup, page 30.
Bottom photo: Rice Mold with Zucchini Band, page 165.

Frozen Lemon Tower (and variation), page 215.

Glamorous Chocolate Mousse Cake, page 204.

Herb Crusted Loin of Lamb, page 102, Spinach Timbale with Gorgonzola, page 190, and Honey Glazed Carrots, page 173.

Seafood

Crab Cakes with Corn   134
Jalapeño Tartar Sauce

Sautéed Flounder   135
Ginger Soy Sauce with Green Onion *

Orange Roughy Veracruzana *   136
Tomatillo Sauce *
Tomato Sauce with Green Chiles *

Lobster Burritos   137
Yellow Tomato Salsa

Red Corn and Chile Crusted Redfish   138
Poblano Vinaigrette

Salmon with Pesto Crust   139
Basil Vinaigrette

Redfish or Trout Fillets *   140
Orange, Tomato, and Cilantro Sauce

Seared Salmon   141
Red Pepper Sauce *
Black Bean Sauce *

Shrimp Enchiladas   142

Grilled Swordfish *   143
Yellow Pepper Sauce

Seared Tuna with Sesame Seeds *   144
Cilantro Vinaigrette
Ginger Vinaigrette

denotes a low fat dish

Crab Cakes with Corn
Jalapeño Tartar Sauce

SERVES 4-6

*It seems no cookbook would be complete without a recipe for
crab cakes. This version combines the flavors of our Texas Gulf
Coast with those of our neighbor, Mexico.*

1/4 cup mayonnaise
2 eggs
1/3 cup frozen corn, defrosted
1/4 cup diced red bell pepper
1/4 cup canned chopped,
   green chiles
2 tablespoons diced red onion
1 teaspoon Dijon mustard
1 tablespoon Worcestershire
Cayenne
1 pound white lump crabmeat
1-2 cups fresh breadcrumbs
4 tablespoons oil
4 tablespoons butter

CRAB CAKES: Place mayonnaise, eggs, corn, red bell pepper, green chiles, red onion, mustard, Worcestershire, and cayenne in a mixing bowl. Stir together to combine well. Pick over crabmeat carefully. Fold crabmeat into other ingredients. Add enough bread crumbs so patties hold shape, about 1/4 cup. Form mixture into patties. Roll crab cakes in fresh breadcrumbs. Refrigerate until ready to serve. Sauté crab cakes in skillet in equal parts oil and butter until nicely browned.

2 cups mayonnaise
3 tablespoons chopped red
   onion
2 tablespoons seeded and
   chopped jalapeños
3 tablespoons chopped
   cornichons
1 tablespoon lemon juice

JALAPEÑO TARTAR SAUCE: Combine mayonnaise, red onion, jalapeños, cornichons, and lemon juice in a mixing bowl. Refrigerate until ready to serve.

TO SERVE: Sauté crab cakes immediately before serving or sauté ahead and reheat on baking sheet in 350°F oven. Serve on plate with jalapeño tartar sauce.

VARIATION: These would also be good served with some of the other sauces and vinaigrettes listed in this book. For example, Cream of Red Bell Pepper Sauce (page 110), Cilantro Vinaigrette (page 144), or Chile Ancho Vinaigrette (page 69).

Sautéed Flounder
Ginger Soy Sauce with Green Onion

This is a light dish that incorporates ginger and soy sauce. It is easier to cook "lighter" when you use good, strong spices. I have not meant for this to be totally low fat, but it can be made such by sautéeing with non-stick cooking spray instead of oil and butter. I have used cornstarch to make the sauce. This makes it possible to prepare the sauce long before you sauté the fish. It also allows you to have a sauce that will be thick but not high in fat content.

---

2 tablespoons butter
2 tablespoons oil
1 pound flounder or orange
    roughy fillets
1 cup flour, seasoned with salt
    and pepper

FILLETS: Melt butter and oil in medium skillet. Wash and dry fillets. Coat lightly in seasoned flour. Sauté fillets on each side until lightly browned, about 2 minutes per side. Timing will depend on thickness of fillets.

3/4 cup white wine
2 tablespoons ginger, minced
1-2 cloves garlic, minced
1/3 cup green onion, chopped
1/4 cup soy sauce
1/2 cup clam juice
1 tablespoon cornstarch
1 tablespoon water

GINGER SOY SAUCE: Put 3/4 cup white wine in small saucepan. Add ginger, garlic, and green onion. Bring to boil. Simmer 5 minutes or until liquid is reduced by half. Add soy sauce and clam juice to reduced wine. Heat. Dissolve cornstarch in water. Add to hot wine-clam juice mixture. Heat until thickened, stirring constantly. Once mixture is thick, do not boil again. Reserve sauce until ready to use.

1/4 cup green onion, chopped

TO SERVE: If not serving immediately, reheat in preheated 350°F oven for 10 minutes. Place on serving platter. Decoratively pour sauce over top. Sprinkle with chopped green onion.

NOTE: *This sauce would be good on any white fleshed fish. Use it also on scallops, shrimp or tuna. It would overpower salmon.*

Orange Roughy Veracruzana
Tomatillo Sauce
Tomato Sauce with Green Chiles

SERVES 4-6

Paesano's is a wonderful Italian restaurant in San Antonio. The owner, Joe Cosniac, has developed many recipes that are not Italian but that are popular with the local clientele. This is one of my favorite low fat dishes which was inspired by one of his specialties.

---

6 orange roughy fillets
Salt and freshly ground black
  pepper
1/4 cup olive oil

FILLETS: Wash and dry fish fillets. Season outside with salt and freshly ground black pepper. Put oil in skillet or grill pan. Sauté fish until tender, 2-3 minutes per side. Reserve on baking sheet if not serving immediately

---

10-15 medium tomatillos,
  peeled and washed
1 serrano pepper, charred and
  seeded
1/3 cup chicken broth
1/2 cup chopped onion
1/2 cup cilantro, stems removed
1 teaspoon salt
1/2 cup water

TOMATILLO SAUCE: Cook tomatillos in boiling water until tender, about 3-5 minutes. Drain. Tomatillos will lose their bright green color when done. Char serrano pepper in skillet or under broiler. Drop into cold water. Peel and seed as best possible. Chop. (You may want to use gloves when handling serrano peppers. They are very hot.) Put 1/3 cup broth in small saucepan. Add onion and sauté until soft, adding additional broth if needed. Put tomatillos, serrano peppers, onion, and cilantro in blender. Season with salt and blend. Add 1/2 cup water or additional broth if necessary to thin down sauce. Purée in blender or leave chunky as you prefer. Can be made ahead.

3/4 cup chopped onion
3 cloves garlic, chopped
1/3-1/2 cup chicken broth
3 10-ounce cans diced tomatoes
  with peppers, drained (Ro-tel)
2 tablespoons tomato paste
1 teaspoon oregano
Salt to taste
1/2 cup water

TOMATO SAUCE: Put onion and garlic in medium saucepan with broth. Sauté until tender, about 5 minutes. Add tomatoes, tomato paste, and oregano. Cook 20-30 minutes or until mixture is thick. Add salt to taste. Purée or leave chunky as you prefer. Can be made ahead.

1/3 cup chopped cilantro,
  for garnish

TO SERVE: Reheat fillets at 350°F, approximately 10 minutes. Place cooked, warm fillets on serving platter. Cover one side of fillets with green tomatillo sauce and other side with red sauce. Sprinkle with cilantro, if desired.

Lobster Burritos
Yellow Tomato Salsa

MAKES 18 BURRITOS

*This is an exciting and colorful dish that makes a wonderful lunch
or a nice first course for an elegant dinner. If serving for lunch,
allow two per person and perhaps bake them in individual
gratin dishes. For a first course, serve one per person.*

4 pounds fresh lobster, cooked
(2-3 lobsters)
1/3 cup olive oil
2-3 garlic cloves, minced
4-6 green onions, chopped
1/2 cup chopped yellow bell
pepper
1/2 cup chopped red bell
pepper
1 serrano pepper, chopped
and seeded
1 14 1/2-ounce can tomatoes,
chopped and drained
1 teaspoon cumin
Salt and pepper
Flour tortillas
Monterey Jack cheese, grated

LOBSTER: Most large grocery stores sell live lobsters and will cook them for you while you do your shopping. If not, bring large pot of water to a boil. Season water with lots of salt–to resemble sea water. When water is at a rolling boil, plunge in lobsters. Let water return to second boil and reduce the heat to a simmer. Continue to cook lobsters, 4 minutes per pound. When cooked, remove from water and allow to cool at room temperature. Split lobster down the back, from head to tail. Remove intestinal vein running from head to tail and small sac behind head. Remove meat from body and claws. Chop and reserve.

FILLING: Place olive oil in 3-quart sauté pan. Add garlic, green onions, yellow and red peppers, and serrano and sauté about 5 minutes over low heat. Add tomatoes, cumin, salt, and pepper to taste. Continue to sauté over moderately high heat until vegetables are tender and almost all liquid has evaporated. Add reserved, chopped lobster meat. Put 1-2 tablespoons filling into a flour tortilla. Sprinkle 1-2 tablespoons grated Monterey Jack cheese over filling and roll up.

1/3 cup olive oil
1 onion, chopped
2-3 cloves garlic, chopped
2 yellow tomatoes, chopped
1/2 cup chopped cilantro
1 cup chicken broth
2 cups heavy cream
1 box small yellow tomatoes,
pear shaped, if possible

2-3 cups grated Monterey Jack
cheese

YELLOW TOMATO SAUCE: Place olive oil in another 3-quart sauté pan. Add onion, garlic, and tomatoes. Sauté until vegetables are tender. Add cilantro, chicken broth, and cream. Turn heat to moderately high and cook until sauce is reduced and thick, about 15-20 minutes. After sauce is thick, add some whole, baby yellow tomatoes for effect.

TO ASSEMBLE AND SERVE: Preheat oven to 350°F. Place filled flour tortillas in individual au gratin dishes or in a large oven proof baking dish with some sauce on bottom. Top with additional sauce and cheese. Bake for 10-20 minutes or until heated through.

Red Corn and Chile Crusted Redfish
Poblano Vinaigrette

SERVES 6

I experimented with this recipe after reading an article in Food and Arts. *I credit the original recipe to Bobby Flay of the Mesa Grill in New York City. I use it to demonstrate the current trend of using room temperature vinaigrettes instead of heavy sauces to compliment certain dishes. This is a nice change for the summer.*

---

10 red corn tortillas
3-4 cups vegetable oil
1/4 cup red chili powder
1/4 cup ground cumin

COATING: Cut tortillas into quarters. Heat oil in small sauté pan until hot but not smoking. Cook tortillas in batches until crisp. Drain on paper towels. Put crisp tortillas and spices in food processor. Grind until smooth. Set aside in mixing bowl.

---

6 redfish or catfish fillets,
   skin removed
Salt and freshly ground
   black pepper
2-3 eggs
Vegetable oil

FILLETS: Wash and dry fillets. Be sure all skin and bones are removed. Season fillets with salt and freshly ground black pepper. Place eggs in mixing bowl. Lightly beat with whisk. Dip fish into eggs. Coat with reserved ground tortilla mixture. Put vegetable oil in large skillet. Heat until hot but not smoking. Sauté fish on both sides, about 3-4 minutes per side, until cooked through. Place on baking sheet if not using right away.

---

2 poblano peppers
Juice of 2 limes
1/2 teaspoon oregano
1 tablespoon light corn syrup
1/3 cup red wine vinegar
1-1 1/3 cups olive oil
Salt and freshly ground
   black pepper

POBLANO VINAIGRETTE: Broil poblano peppers on all sides until charred. Wrap in a tea towel to cool. Peel and seed when cool enough to handle. Do not be too meticulous about removing the peel. Poblanos do not need to be peeled perfectly. Put the poblano peppers, lime juice, oregano, corn syrup, and red wine vinegar in blender and blend until smooth. With machine running, pour in the oil through feed tube. Season with salt and freshly ground black pepper.

TO SERVE: Reheat fillets in 350°F oven for 5-10 minutes. Place on individual plates or serving platter. Serve with Poblano Vinaigrette.

NOTES: If you can find packaged fried red corn tortillas at a local grocery store, use them and eliminate the first step. The fillets look beautiful served on a bed of fresh spinach.

Salmon with Pesto Crust
Basil Vinaigrette

SERVES 8

I truly think you will find this to be one of the best recipes for salmon. It was inspired by a recipe in Food and Wine.

1/2 cup fresh basil leaves
2 cloves garlic
2 strips bacon, uncooked
1 1/2 cups bread crumbs, fresh
1/3 cup Parmesan cheese, freshly grated
1/4 cup olive oil

PESTO: Put basil, garlic, and bacon in processor. Process until minced and well combined. Add bread crumbs and Parmesan cheese. With machine running, pour olive oil in through feed tube. Mixture should be moist enough to stick to fish, but not runny.

1 large salmon fillet, skin removed, and cut into two large pieces
Salt and freshly ground black pepper
Olive oil

SALMON: Have the butcher give you one side of a whole salmon with the skin removed. Wash and dry salmon fillet. Season fillet on both sides with salt and freshly ground black pepper. Spread flesh side of salmon (as opposed to side that had skin attached) with pesto. Press pesto down to be sure it adheres to flesh. Coat grill pan lightly with oil. Heat pan until very hot. Add salmon, pesto side down. Grill for 3 minutes or until pesto is crisp and brown. Turn fillet over and cook 2-3 more minutes. If not serving immediately, put fillet on baking sheet and set aside. Just before serving, reheat in preheated 350°F oven.

1/3 cup red wine vinegar
1/2 cup fresh basil
2 cloves garlic
1 tablespoon Dijon mustard
Salt and freshly ground black pepper
1-1 1/2 cups olive oil

BASIL VINAIGRETTE: Put vinegar, basil, garlic, Dijon mustard, salt, and pepper in food processor. Process until ingredients are minced. With machine on, add oil through feed tube. Mixture will emulsify or become thick. Correct seasoning. Serve at room temperature.

TO SERVE: Place salmon on serving dish and serve with vinaigrette or sauce of your choice. I often use Red Bell Pepper Sauce.

Redfish or Trout Fillets
Orange, Tomato, and Cilantro Sauce

My father's family was originally from the Gulf Coast. Because of this, every summer of my childhood was spent in Rockport, Texas. Crab, fish and oysters were a part of our daily life, both in the catching and in the eating. I still love seafood and serve it often. If redfish or trout is not available, buy orange roughy or another firm white fish to prepare this dish.

---

1 1/2 pounds redfish or trout fillets (approximately 4-5 fillets)

Flour, seasoned with salt and freshly ground black pepper

4 tablespoons oil

4 tablespoons butter

Juice of 1 lemon

FILLETS: Wash fillets and pat dry. Dust lightly with seasoned flour. Put oil and butter in large skillet. When butter begins to sizzle, sauté fish fillets over medium high heat, 2-3 minutes on each side. Fish should be browned nicely. Sprinkle lemon juice over fish.

1/2 cup fresh orange juice

1/2 cup peeled, diced tomatoes

2-3 cloves garlic, minced

1 tablespoon chopped shallots

2 tablespoons chopped cilantro

1/2 cup white wine

1 stick butter, room temperature, cut into 8 tablespoons

Salt and freshly ground black pepper

SAUCE: Place orange juice, tomatoes, garlic, shallots, cilantro, and wine in small saucepan. Simmer until reduced to 3-4 tablespoons, about 10 minutes. Remove from heat and add butter, 1 tablespoon at a time, beating well after each addition. Mixture will become thick. Season with salt and freshly ground black pepper. Keep warm over hot water.

TO SERVE: Serve fish immediately topped with sauce, or sauté ahead and reheat in 350°F oven for 10 minutes.

Seared Salmon
Red Pepper Sauce
Black Bean Sauce

SERVES 8-10

Salmon served on a bed of these two low fat sauces makes a beautiful presentation. This dish can be served to anyone on a restricted diet or at an elegant dinner. I submitted this recipe to the Cancer Therapy and Research Center's newsletter as a healthy, low fat dish.

1 large salmon fillet, skinned
Salt and freshly ground
   black pepper
Olive oil
Juice of 1 lemon

SALMON: Wash and dry salmon. Remove small bones running down salmon's back with tweezers. Salt and pepper both sides of fillet. Lightly oil grill pan. Sauté salmon over high heat for 4-5 minutes on each side. Begin cooking on side that had skin attached. Sprinkle with lemon juice. Salmon can be undercooked and finished in 350°F oven for 10 minutes.

2 red bell peppers, peeled
   and seeded
2 red chiles colorados or
   chiles anchos
1-2 cups water
2 tablespoons oil
1/4 cup onion, chopped
2 cloves garlic, chopped
3/4-1 cup chicken broth

RED PEPPER SAUCE: Roast red peppers under broiler flame. Cool in tea towel. Peel and seed. Boil chiles colorados or chiles anchos in small amount of water until soft, about 5 minutes. Drain. Heat oil in small saucepan. Add onion and garlic. Sauté until tender. When soft, place onion and garlic into blender with red bell peppers and softened chiles colorados or chiles anchos. Add broth. Blend until smooth. Add additional broth to reach desired consistency.

1/4 cup olive oil
1-2 serrano peppers, seeded
   and chopped
1/3 cup onion, chopped
1 large garlic clove, chopped
1/2 cup cilantro
1 15-ounce can black beans,
   not drained
1-2 cups chicken broth
Salt

BLACK BEAN SAUCE: Heat oil in small saucepan. Add serrano peppers, onion, and garlic. Sauté until tender. Remove vegetables to blender. Add cilantro, black beans, and 1/2 of broth. Purée in blender with vegetables. Add additional broth to reach desired consistency. Season with salt. Sauce can be made several days ahead and reheated.

Fresh cilantro

TO SERVE: Reheat sauces. Put some of each sauce on individual plates. Cut salmon into individual servings and place on plates atop two sauces. Sprinkle with fresh cilantro.

Shrimp Enchiladas

SERVES 10-12

The idea for this recipe came from Paul Prudhomme. Everything can be made and completely put together the day before serving. Bake immediately before serving. The enchiladas may be served in one large baking dish or individual gratin dishes.

1/2 stick butter
1 onion, chopped
2 4-ounce cans chopped
   green chiles
1 green bell pepper, chopped
3 cloves garlic, chopped
1 teaspoon oregano
1/2 teaspoon cayenne
Salt and pepper
3 cups heavy cream
1 cup sour cream

SAUCE: Melt butter in 3-quart sauté pan. Add onion, green chiles, green bell pepper, garlic, oregano, and cayenne. Simmer ingredients until tender, about 10 minutes. Season with salt and pepper. Add cream to vegetables. Bring to boil. Simmer 10 minutes. Add sour cream. Heat gently until sour cream is incorporated. Once you have added sour cream, do not boil.

1/2 stick butter
1 bunch green onions, chopped
1 teaspoon cayenne
1 teaspoon oregano
2 pounds shrimp, peeled and
   cut into 1/4-inch dice
Salt

FILLING: Melt butter in saucepan. Add onions, cayenne, and oregano. Cook onions until tender, about 10 minutes. Add shrimp. Simmer about 3 minutes or until shrimp is just done. Add 1 cup sauce to shrimp mixture.

2-3 cups vegetable oil
20 corn tortillas
Shrimp filling
1-2 cups mozzarella cheese,
   grated

TO ASSEMBLE: Put vegetable oil in small skillet. Heat until very hot. Dip tortillas into hot oil for 5-10 seconds. Drain. Soft fry tortillas one at a time. You may stack them after cooking. Put small amount of sauce on bottom of baking dish or individual gratin dishes. When cool enough to handle, put 1-2 tablespoons filling in each tortilla along with 1 tablespoon mozzarella cheese. Roll up. Place seam side down in baking dish or dishes. Cover enchiladas with remaining sauce. Top with remaining grated cheese.

TO SERVE: Bake in preheated 350°F oven for 20 minutes or until hot and cheese is lightly browned. You may want to broil for final browning, about 2-3 minutes.

VARIATION: *Substitute Swiss or Monterey Jack for mozzarella.*

Grilled Swordfish
Yellow Pepper Sauce

*This recipe was given to me by a childhood friend and former owner
of Pace Foods. It was served at a dinner where all the dishes included
Pace Picante Sauce. I found this dish to be tasty and beautiful. The
pale yellow color with small swirls of picante is impressive.*

6 swordfish steaks, 3/4-inch
   thick and skinless
Salt and freshly ground
   black pepper
Olive oil

SWORDFISH STEAKS: Preheat oven to 350°F. Wash and dry swordfish steaks. Salt and pepper both sides. Lightly oil grill pan and grill steaks on each side until done, about 3-4 minutes per side. If not using immediately, undercook fish slightly and place on baking sheet. Before serving, reheat for 10 minutes in 350°F oven.

3 yellow bell peppers
1/2 cup chicken broth
1/4 cup dry white wine
2 tablespoons flour
1 shallot, minced
2 cloves garlic, minced
2 cups heavy cream
Juice of 1/2 lemon
Salt and pepper
Chicken broth or clam juice

YELLOW PEPPER SAUCE: Broil peppers until charred on all sides. Place in paper bag or tea towel and cool. Peel and seed. This is easy to do under cold running water. Place peppers, broth, wine, flour, shallots, and garlic in blender. Process at high speed until smooth. Pour pepper mixture into 3-quart sauté pan. Add cream and lemon juice. Cook over medium heat, about 5 minutes or until thickened. Season to taste. Thin with chicken broth or clam juice if necessary.

1/2 cup Pace Picante Sauce
Fresh cilantro

TO ASSEMBLE AND SERVE AS SEPARATE FISH COURSE: Cut steaks into neat squares. One steak should make two first course servings. Cover large dinner plate with sauce. Place one warm steak in center. Place 5 spoonfuls of picante sauce equally spaced around fish on sauce. Draw a knife through picante sauce to make abstract design. Garnish with fresh cilantro.

TO ASSEMBLE AND SERVE AS PART OF A MEAL: Place sauce on large platter. Top with warm steaks. Dot sauce with Pace Picante. Garnish with cilantro.

NOTES: Sauce can be made ahead and kept covered in refrigerator. Reheat before serving. When grilling fish, do not turn it back and forth. To get good grill markings, leave fish on one side for 3-4 minutes. Don't peek. Turn over and do other side. This is also true for meat.

Seared Tuna with Sesame Seeds
Cilantro Vinaigrette
Ginger Vinaigrette

SERVES 6

Tuna is best cooked rare and served sliced on the diagonal. This recipe is for rare tuna, but feel free to cook it longer if you prefer. I am suggesting two vinaigrettes that go well with the tuna. In the summer, serve the tuna with one or both of these as a main course. Serve vinaigrettes at room temperature. You may also use this to accompany salad greens as a light lunch .

6 1-inch thick tuna fillets, about 8-ounces each, skin removed
Salt and freshly ground black pepper
4-6 tablespoons olive oil
1 cup sesame seeds

FILLETS: Wash and dry tuna fillets. Season both sides of fillets with salt and freshly ground black pepper. Brush with olive oil. Coat both sides generously with sesame seeds, pressing them into fillets with your hands. Lightly coat a medium skillet with additional olive oil and heat until hot. Sear tuna over high heat for 2 minutes per side for rare tuna. Serve with one or both vinaigrettes.

1/2 cup cilantro
2 cloves garlic
1/3 cup vinegar
1 teaspoon Dijon mustard
1 cup olive oil
Salt and freshly ground black pepper

CILANTRO VINAIGRETTE: Place cilantro and garlic in food processor. Process until minced. Add vinegar and Dijon mustard. Process. With machine running, add oil through feed tube. Season with salt and freshly ground black pepper.

1 1-inch piece of fresh ginger, peeled
2 cloves garlic
1 teaspoon fresh rosemary
1/3 cup white wine vinegar
2 tablespoons soy sauce
1 tablespoon honey
1 cup olive oil
2-3 drops sesame oil
Salt and freshly ground black pepper

GINGER VINAIGRETTE: Place ginger, garlic, and rosemary in food processor. Process to mince. Add vinegar, soy sauce, and honey. Process quickly. With machine running add olive oil and sesame oil through feed tube. Continue processing until mixture is emulsified. Season to taste.

144

Starches

Creamed Fresh Corn   147

Corn Pudding   148

Ida's Cornbread Dressing   149

Couscous with Peas and Red Peppers   150

Fettuccine Alfredo   151

Homemade Pasta   152

Stuffed Pasta Shells with Tomato Sauce *   153

Pasta with Corn and Red Pepper   154

Fideo   155

Parmesan Grits with Green Chiles   156

Polenta Fritters or Polenta Sautéed   157

Polenta with Four Cheeses   158

Potatoes Anna   159

Fried Potato Baskets   160

Potatoes au Gratin Mexican Style   161

Potatoes Supreme or Potatoes Salieu   162

Two Potato and Onion Cake   163

— *continued on next page* —

Starches

— continued —

Potato and Wild Mushroom Napoleons   164

Rice Mold with Zucchini Band   165

Baked Four Grain Dressing   166

Rice Pilaf   167

Purée of White Bean and Potato   168

* denotes a low fat dish

Creamed Fresh Corn

Some of the simplest dishes are the best and this corn is proof. I have never served this dish that it has not met with rave reviews. It is an old family recipe that will never go out of style. I especially use it in the summer when corn is sweet and fresh. It is inexpensive and delightful. I serve it with casual meals such as barbecued chicken, but I also do not hesitate to serve it at a fancy dinner party.

1 stick butter
12 ears corn, shucks removed
4 cups half and half or enough
   to barely cover corn
1 corn cob, corn removed
Salt and pepper

CORN: Melt butter in large, deep pot. Remove corn from cob by scraping it off with large knife. Scrape deep into cobs as they contain good juice and starch. Sauté corn in butter over moderate heat for 10 minutes. Add half and half, corn cob and seasonings. Bring to a boil. Reduce heat to simmer. Cook until corn is crisp-tender, about 30 minutes. Season well.

TO SERVE: Reheat on top of stove. Remove cob and serve in large serving bowl.

NOTES: *For some reason, corn cooked in this fashion can be reheated and never lose its crispness. Since this is "classic country," season with lots of pepper.*

Corn Pudding

SERVES 6-8

This is a typical Southern dish that is great for fall menus.

2 tablespoons butter
3/4 cup chopped onion
2 cloves garlic, chopped
3 cups frozen corn, defrosted
4 eggs
2 tablespoons flour
1 tablespoon parsley
1 teaspoon sugar
1/2 cup heavy cream
1/2 cup half and half cream
Salt and pepper
Pinch of cayenne

CORN PUDDING: Preheat oven to 350°F. Melt butter in small sauté pan. Add onion and garlic. Sauté until tender, about 5 minutes. Reserve in mixing bowl. Cool. Purée 2 cups corn in food processor. Put in mixing bowl with onion mixture. Add remaining cup of whole corn. Mix eggs, flour, parsley, sugar, and creams into corn mixture. Season with salt, pepper, and cayenne. Pour into an 11x7x1 1/2-inch baking dish. Bake until set, about 1 hour. This is best baked just before it is served; however, it can be cut into slices and reheated in foil for 15 minutes at 350°F.

TO SERVE: Serve directly from baking dish, or cut into individual servings and place on platter.

NOTES: I have reheated corn pudding in a microwave and the taste and texture are fine. This recipe doubles easily and makes for a more spectacular presentation. Bake in a deep dish and it will puff up slightly.

Ida's Cornbread Dressing

SERVES 20

I have discovered that holiday traditions are hard to break. My grandmother made this dressing for me as a child. I cannot imagine a Thanksgiving without it. The moral is to be careful what you first serve your children at these special times. Any change will be unacceptable.

1 stick butter

2 large yellow onions, chopped

2 bunches green onions, chopped

8 stalks celery, chopped (or 1 bunch)

3 green bell peppers, chopped

4-6 cups chicken broth

Huge pan of corn bread (made from 6 6-ounce packages yellow corn meal if using packaged mixes)

5 eggs, hardboiled and chopped

2 4-ounce jars pimento, chopped

Salt and pepper

1 stick butter or some pan drippings from cooked turkey

DRESSING: Melt butter in 5-quart sauté pan. Add yellow onions, green onions, celery and green bell peppers. Cook until tender on very slow heat. Vegetables exude quite a bit of juice when sautéed slowly. Heat broth. You may want to spice broth up with a little thyme, onion, bay leaf and celery. Crumble cornbread in large mixing bowl. Add cooked vegetables with their juices. Pour hot broth over cornbread to soften. Stir well, pressing cornbread smooth with back of wooden spoon. Add eggs and pimento. Season well. Add lots of salt and pepper. Add some additional butter, or even better, add some drippings from turkey. This is Thanksgiving after all! Put in baking dish. Refrigerate until ready to serve. Bake 30 minutes in preheated 350°F oven, or reheat on top of stove. Add additional broth if necessary.

VARIATION: *Substitute red bell pepper for pimento. Sauté 2 chopped red bell peppers along with other vegetables.*

NOTE: *The problem with most dressings is that they are not sufficiently moist. Add enough broth to make dressing moist.*

Couscous with Peas and Red Pepper

SERVES 4

*Couscous is a Middle Eastern dish that is very quick to prepare
and extremely versatile as it lends itself to the addition of a wide
variety of herbs and spices.*

1 box couscous

1/4 cup dried currants

2 tablespoons butter

2 tablespoons olive oil

1 red bell pepper, chopped

1 teaspoon ground cumin

1 package frozen peas,
    defrosted

Salt and pepper

2 tablespoons parsley,
    chopped

COUSCOUS: Combine couscous and currants. Cook mixture according to instructions on couscous package. Melt butter and oil in 3-quart sauté pan. Sauté red bell pepper with cumin in butter and oil until tender. Add peppers and defrosted peas to couscous. Season with salt, pepper, and parsley. Add additional cumin if you desire.

TO SERVE: Reheat couscous on top of stove. Place couscous in serving dish or pack into individual 6-ounce ramekins or molds that have been coated with non-stick cooking spray. Reheat molds in 350°F oven for 20 minutes. Unmold by turning out onto serving dish or individual plate. Just give filled, warm mold a sharp rap and couscous will come out easily.

NOTE: *To create a low fat dish, omit butter and olive oil. Sauté peppers in 1/3 cup chicken broth.*

Fettuccine Alfredo

My dad, who ate pasta every Sunday night, created this version of an old favorite. I think the secret ingredient is the Lawry's seasoned salt. Some students disagree and leave it out entirely. Once again feel free to eliminate or add to any recipe. I have one student who suggests using fat free yogurt instead of sour cream and green onion instead of chives. Be creative.

1 pound fettuccine noodles

2 tablespoons salt

6 tablespoons butter

4 cups half and half cream

1 cup sour cream

1/2 cup grated Parmesan
cheese

1/4 cup chopped chives

2 teaspoons Lawry's
seasoned salt

Salt and pepper to taste

FETTUCCINE ALFREDO: Bring water seasoned with salt to boil in large stock pot. Cook pasta until tender, about 8-10 minutes. Drain. Melt butter in 3-quart sauté pan. Add cream and heat. Add sour cream. Stir to heat. Do not boil or sour cream will curdle. Add Parmesan cheese, chives, and seasonings. Add drained fettuccine to cream mixture. If fettuccine needs additional liquid, add milk.

TO SERVE: This can be prepared ahead. Reheat on top of stove, adding additional liquid if necessary. Serve on serving platter or in chafing dish.

NOTE: Everyone thinks pasta must be done at the last minute. I have used this recipe at a catered party for 150 people. Everything was put together around 2 p.m. and reheated just before serving. You will need to add additional liquid, as cooked pasta continues to absorb liquid. Add milk, not additional cream, to precooked fettuccine mixture.

Homemade Pasta

SERVES 6-8

*I am including this recipe for cooks who want to offer guests
something really special. All pasta recipes in this book can be
completed without going to the trouble; however, if time permits,
making homemade pasta is rewarding and fun.*

2 cups flour
3 eggs

DOUGH: Put flour and eggs in food processor. Process until mixture forms ball. Remove dough from food processor, forming it into smooth ball with your hands. If dough is sticky, return to processor and add an additional 1/4 cup flour. Process again. Dough will break apart but do not worry; it will come together again. It is fine to coat outside of dough with some flour, but very little should be needed. If dough sticks while being kneaded, you need additional flour.

KNEADING DOUGH: Keep pasta machine on largest setting or #1 on most pasta machines. While you are kneading you will never change setting. Each time you run dough through machine, it will get wider. To begin kneading dough, run it through machine as many times as it takes for it to reach width of machine. When you have reached width of machine fold in half lengthwise. Repeat same process of running dough through machine, folding in half again when dough reaches width of machine. Do this 4-5 times. The last time it reaches width of machine, do not fold.

STRETCHING PASTA: Now you are ready to make dough skinny. Move setting on machine to #2 and run dough through machine two times. (It may be easier for you to work with only half of dough at a time. If so, cut kneaded dough in half and cover piece you are not immediately using with tea towel.) Dough will no longer get wider. It will only get longer. After you have run dough through twice on setting #2, move setting to #3 and run dough through two times again. Change setting to #4 and repeat process. Change setting to #5 and repeat process. At this time you may feel dough is thin enough. If so, cut long strips into sections and make ravioli or any shape of pasta.

COOKING PASTA: To cook pasta, bring large pot of salted water to boil and boil pasta for several minutes. Fresh pasta cooks much faster than dried pasta.

Stuffed Pasta Shells with Tomato Sauce

Serves 6-8

*This tomato sauce is wonderful and may be used in
many other pasta dishes.*

20-25 large pasta shells,
    plus some extra to allow
    for breakage
1/3 cup olive oil

PASTA: Cook pasta according to instructions on box. Drain. Allow to cool sufficiently so they can be handled. Reserve. Toss with small amount of olive oil to keep pasta from sticking together. Cool until ready to stuff.

1/2 stick butter
4 green onions, chopped
2 cloves garlic, minced
2 packages frozen, chopped
    spinach, defrosted
1/2 pound ricotta cheese
1/2 pound prosciutto,
    cut into small cubes or
    diced in food processor
1/2 cup grated Parmesan cheese
Salt and pepper

FILLING: Melt butter in 3-quart sauté pan. Add green onion and garlic. Sauté until tender. Squeeze out all excess moisture from spinach. Add to sautéed onion and garlic. Mix well and remove to mixing bowl. Stir in ricotta, prosciutto, and Parmesan cheese. Season to taste.

2 tablespoons olive oil
2 cloves garlic, minced
3/4 cup minced onion
1 28-ounce can whole tomatoes
3 tablespoons balsamic vinegar
2 tablespoons tomato paste
1/4 cup chopped fresh basil
2 tablespoons fresh parsley,
    minced
1 teaspoon dried oregano or
    2 tablespoons fresh oregano
1 bay leaf

TOMATO SAUCE: Heat olive oil in medium saucepan. Add garlic and onion. Sauté until vegetables are tender. Roughly chop tomatoes. Add tomatoes, balsamic vinegar, tomato paste, fresh basil, parsley, oregano and bay leaf. Cook over moderately low heat, for 45 minutes to 1 hour. Remove bay leaf. Purée in blender or food processor, or leave chunky if you wish.

1-2 cups grated mozzarella
1/2 cup grated Parmesan
Olive oil

TO ASSEMBLE AND SERVE: Preheat oven to 350°F. Stuff pasta shells with filling. Place stuffed pasta shells in a 13x9-inch baking dish in one layer. Cover with tomato sauce. Generously sprinkle with mozzarella and Parmesan. Drizzle with olive oil. Bake for 30 minutes or until cheese is melted and sauce is bubbling.

Pasta with Corn and Red Pepper

SERVES 8-10

I created this recipe for a Southwest class. It is so simple that it is hard to believe the taste is so wonderful, not to mention the striking color.

3 tablespoons butter
3 tablespoons olive oil
2 red bell peppers, chopped
2 cloves garlic, minced
1 1-pound package fettuccine
  noodles
1 1-pound package frozen
  corn, defrosted
6 tablespoons olive oil
Salt and freshly ground
  black pepper
1/2 cup chopped cilantro
  (optional)

PASTA: Melt butter with olive oil in small skillet. Add peppers and garlic. Cook until tender but still slightly crunchy, about 5 minutes. Bring large pot of salted water to boil. Cook pasta until tender. Drain. Add red bell peppers with butter and olive oil to pasta. Add corn. Season with salt and freshly ground black pepper. Season with cilantro if you desire.

TO SERVE: Serve on large platter or on individual plates as a side dish. (This dish accompanies the grilled salmon in the photogragh on page 124.)

VARIATIONS: If you like the two colors but want a change, use a mixture of red and yellow peppers instead of corn. Do not use green bell peppers. The taste will be too strong. Substitute fresh basil for cilantro and fresh, chopped tomatoes for corn. Try using sautéed zucchini. Change this simple dish to suit your mood.

Fideo

This is a valuable recipe which is not found in many cook books. It is a good, unusual starch. It is often served with Mexican meals but would be a good accompaniment to any meat grilled outside.

1/4 cup oil or bacon grease

2-3 cloves garlic, chopped

1 onion, chopped

1 large potato, peeled and chopped

2 5-ounce packages vermicelli or fideo noodles

1 tablespoon cumin

5 cups water

1 tablespoon Caldo de Pollo seasoning or 1 chicken bouillon cube

Salt and pepper to taste

FIDEO: Heat oil or bacon grease until hot but not smoking in 5-quart sauté pan. Add garlic, onion and potato pieces. Sauté, stirring often, for 5-10 minutes or until potatoes begin to soften. Add fideo noodles. (Vermicelli noodles are fideo noodles.) Break up noodles with your hands or with spoon. Sauté noodles over moderately high heat until browned, stirring often. Add cumin. Add enough water to barely cover noodles. Add bouillon cube or Caldo de Pollo seasoning. Simmer, uncovered, 8-10 minutes or until noodles are cooked and liquid has almost totally evaporated. Do not stir. Adjust seasoning. Be sure you have enough cumin to impart a robust flavor. It is cumin that gives fideo its character.

TO SERVE: Adjust seasoning. Reheat on top of stove. You may need to add a small amount of broth or water to reheat. Serve on attractive platter.

NOTES: Do not overcook or fideo will become gummy. Do not add too much water during the initial cooking. You want noodles to cook and water to evaporate simultaneously. You can buy vermicelli noodles already broken up. They will probably be sold as fideo noodles. Caldo de Pollo seasoning can be found in the Mexican food section of most grocery stores. It is a staple in homes that often serve Mexican food.

Parmesan Grits with Green Chiles

As a native Texan, I could not write a book that did not include grits. Actually, grits are a version of polenta, which is currently very popular. They can be treated exactly the same. Grits can be kept soft by adding additional liquid after they are cooked or they can be put in glass baking dish and allowed to cool and harden. When hard, they can be cut into desired shape and sautéed as you would polenta. Today there are wonderful stone ground grits on the market. Look around. You can make this traditional southern dish into something fancy and new.

---

2 cups milk
2 cups water
1 teaspoon salt
1 cup regular grits
1/2 stick butter
1/4 cup chopped parsley
1 4-ounce can chopped
  green chiles
1/2 cup grated Parmesan
  cheese
1/2 cup grated Cheddar cheese
1/2 cup milk or
  half and half cream
Cayenne and salt to taste

GRITS: Heat milk, water, and salt in 3-quart sauté pan until boiling. Add grits. Lower heat to simmer and cook grits until thickened. Add butter, parsley, green chiles, cheeses, and milk. Heat until cheese is melted and grits are smooth. Season with cayenne and salt.

Grated Parmesan cheese
Grated Cheddar cheese

TO SERVE: Serve immediately or place in glass baking dish, top with additional cheeses and bake in preheated 350°F oven for 30 minutes or until hot.

Polenta Fritters
Polenta Sautéed

SERVES 8-10

Polenta is an excellent starch as it can be prepared so many ways–
creamy, cheesy, sautéed or fried. Use instant polenta to
make this very easy.

8 cups water seasoned with
  1 1/2 tablespoons salt
2 2/3 cups yellow corn meal
3 eggs
1 cup flour seasoned with
  1/2 teaspoon salt and pepper
1 cup fresh bread crumbs
Olive oil

POLENTA FRITTERS: Bring salted water to boil in large stock pot. When water is boiling, add cornmeal in slow, steady stream while stirring. You can keep lumps from forming by slowly adding cornmeal, stirring at all times. Once cornmeal is added, reduce heat to low and cook, stirring constantly, until polenta is very thick and pulls away from side of pan, 25-30 minutes. Once thick, transfer to a 15x10x2-inch ovenproof pan sprayed with a non-stick cooking spray and spread in 1/4-inch thick layer. At this point, you may cover polenta and refrigerate overnight. Use biscuit or cookie cutter to cut cold polenta into shapes or rounds about 2 inches in diameter. Allow 2 per person. Beat eggs lightly in mixing bowl. Place seasoned flour and bread crumbs into two additional mixing bowls. Dip polenta rounds in flour, then in egg, then in bread crumbs. Cover bottom of 3-quart sauté pan with olive oil, about 1/4 cup, and heat. Add as many polenta pieces as you can in one layer. Sauté on both sides until browned nicely, about 2-3 minutes over moderately high heat. You may need to add additional oil as you sauté second and third batches of polenta.

TO SERVE: Serve immediately or place on baking sheet and reheat in 350°F oven for 10 minutes or until hot. Serve as a side dish with your choice of entrée.

POLENTA SAUTÉED: Sauté plain cut rounds in olive oil until brown on each side. If meal is plated in the kitchen, these make wonderful mounds on which to lay a piece of fish or meat. Otherwise, they are just great served as a side dish.

VARIATION: Place a filling such as goat cheese between two pieces of polenta, fry and serve. These would be nice on top of green salad. For an extra flourish, add some fresh basil to the goat cheese. It would make a nice lunch with a cup of soup.

Polenta with Four Cheeses

SERVES 8-10

This preparation of polenta is much like preparing a casserole. It can be assembled the day before needed and reheated immediately before serving. This is an Italian classic!

3 cups milk
2 cups water
1 1/2 cups yellow cornmeal
1 teaspoon salt

POLENTA: Combine milk and water in 3-quart sauté pan. Mix 1 cup of milk-water mixture with cornmeal and salt. Bring remaining 4 cups of milk-water to boil. Reduce heat to low. Slowly stir in cornmeal mixture with wire whisk. Whisk until smooth. Continue to cook, stirring with wooden spoon, until it is thick and you can see bottom of pan when stirring, about 10-15 minutes.

1/2 cup grated Parmesan
1 cup grated mozzarella
1 1/2 cups ricotta
1/2 cup crumbled Gorgonzola
Additional Parmesan cheese
1/2 stick melted butter

TO ASSEMBLE AND SERVE: Preheat oven to 400°F. Butter 11 3/4x7 1/2x1-inch baking dish. Spread half the polenta into prepared dish. Spread Parmesan, mozzarella, ricotta, and Gorgonzola over top. Spread remaining polenta over cheese mixture. Top with additional Parmesan and melted butter. Bake until cheese begins to brown, about 15 minutes.

VARIATION: Fill middle with fresh cooked spinach and sautéed ham and red bell pepper. Top with tomato sauce. Turn it into a Southwestern dish by filling center with chopped green chiles, Monterey Jack cheese, black beans, and cilantro. Cut into wedges. Serve with Red Pepper Sauce, page 141.

Potatoes Anna

SERVES 8

It is my hope that this cookbook will be one of your most used books. For me to feel assured of this fact, I felt it necessary to include some classic recipes that I use over and over again. This is one of those recipes. Make Potatoes Anna early in the day and reheat them on a baking sheet.

1 stick unsalted butter, melted
4-6 large baking potatoes,
  peeled and thinly sliced
Salt and pepper

POTATOES: Preheat oven to 425°F. Pour 1/4 cup butter into heavy ovenproof, 8-inch skillet and heat over moderately high heat. When butter bubbles, remove from heat. Arrange potatoes in overlapping spiral pattern in skillet. Pour in 1 tablespoon additional butter, salt and pepper. Arrange another layer of overlapping potatoes in a spiral. Continue until all potatoes are used, or until skillet is full of potatoes. Cover with foil and place heavy pan on top to press potatoes down and seal them together. Bake for 50 minutes. Remove cover and cook 15-20 minutes more until top layer is very crisp. Try to loosen potatoes periodically to be sure they will unmold.

TO SERVE: Turn potatoes out on to a serving dish. If prepared ahead, reheat in 350° oven for 15 minutes.

VARIATIONS: Put grated Parmesan cheese, onion slices various herbs, Swiss cheese or zucchini slices between the layers. For a less French version, try layering fresh, chopped basil and sautéed onions and yellow or red bell peppers.

NOTES: As Potatoes Anna bake, they will shrink in size. You will end up with potatoes that are more like a pancake. Small skillets or 2 or 3-inch ring molds can also be used to make individual Potatoes Anna. Put rings on buttered baking sheet. Use small baking potatoes and layer potatoes in same manner as master recipe.

Fried Potato Baskets

For this dish you will need a potato basket fryer, a classic piece of equipment available at most good cooking stores. It is dishes such as this that made me fall in love with the magic of cooking. Fill potato baskets with vegetables or fried potatoes or place basket in center of dinner plate and fill with mixed salad greens. Arrange grilled shrimp, seafood sausage, or crab cakes around plate. Use a variety of vinaigrettes for flavor and decoration.

6 medium white potatoes
Deep soup pot
Potato basket fryer with clasp
Mazola or other vegetable oil

POTATO BASKETS: Allow one medium potato per basket. Peel and shred potatoes using shredder blade of food processor (or a mandoline if you have one). Soak in water if not using right away. Place vegetable oil in a deep soup pot. Use enough oil to totally submerge the potato basket. Heat oil to hot but not smoking. Place potato basket equipment in the oil while oil is heating. Place paper towels on counter. Drain grated potatoes on paper towels. Extract any excess moisture from potatoes with your hands. Remove as much moisture as possible. Lift hot fryer from oil. Fill bottom of fryer with 1/2 cup grated potato and secure top with clasp. Submerge filled basket in hot oil. Fry potatoes until they are cooked throughout and nicely browned. This will take approximately 5 minutes, so arrange the fryer in a pot deep enough so that you can walk away while potatoes are cooking. This will allow you to do something else. When done, try to wiggle free top of fryer from cooked potato basket. If this can not be done fairly easily the potatoes are not cooked sufficiently. In this case, allow them to cook a few more minutes. Try to remove top again. When potatoes are cooked the top will come off quite easily. Once you have removed top part of fryer, look at potato basket. If potatoes appear to be cooked throughout, tap bottom part of fryer, which contains the cooked, shredded potatoes, on counter. The potato basket will fall out easily if you give it quite a tap. Don't worry; it won't break.

TO SERVE: Make potato baskets ahead and store in sealable plastic bags. They may be frozen. Reheat in 300°F oven for 10-15 minutes or until hot before using.

Potatoes au Gratin Mexican Style

SERVES 10-12

I created this dish for a Southwest class. As so often happens, it is based on classic French cuisine. I took a potato au gratin recipe and used red pepper, cilantro and toasted tortillas to change its character.

8 baking potatoes, peeled
1 stick butter
Salt and pepper
1 1/2 quarts half and half cream
1 red bell pepper, chopped
   relatively small
1/3 cup olive oil
8 corn tortillas
4 cups vegetable oil

POTATOES: Preheat oven to 350°F. Cut potatoes into 1/2-inch cubes. Place 1/3 potatoes in buttered baking dish. Top with pats of butter, salt and pepper. Repeat with another 1/3 potatoes, additional pats of butter, salt, and pepper. Finish with last 1/3 potatoes, ending with butter, salt and pepper. Add half and half to cover. Bake for 1 1/2 hours or until potatoes are tender and cream has thickened. Sauté red bell peppers, cut into same size cubes as potatoes, in olive oil until crisp-tender. Reserve. Cut tortillas into very thin strips, 1/4-inch wide. Heat vegetable oil in small sauté pan. You need about 1/2-inch depth of oil. Oil should be very hot, but not smoking. Fry tortillas until crisp, approximately 1-2 minutes. Drain.

1 cup chopped cilantro

To ASSEMBLE AND SERVE: Before serving, mix sautéed peppers and 1 cup chopped cilantro into hot potatoes. Top with toasted tortilla strips. It is possible to combine peppers, potatoes, and cilantro and reheat later in 350°F oven for 30 minutes. Top with tortilla strips before serving.

VARIATIONS: *To make classic au gratins, slice potatoes thinly in rounds instead of cutting into cubes and omit peppers and cilantro. Cheese could be added to change this dish– make it Swiss or Monterey Jack, not a yellow cheese. Omit tortillas, use basil instead of cilantro, and you have an Italian au gratin. Also try using fresh cubed tomatoes instead of peppers.*

Potatoes Supreme
Potatoes Salieu

SERVES 8

These two great recipes demonstrate how so many dishes are derived from classic French cuisine. I taught Potatoes Salieu in a classic French class. My sister, Kathryn, found the Potatoes Supreme recipe in a local newspaper. Both recipes contain the same ingredients, but they seem quite different because of the manner in which they are baked.

---

4 large baking potatoes, peeled
1 stick butter, melted
2 cups half and half cream
1/2 pound yellow cheese, grated
Salt and pepper
1 pint sour cream
1/2 cup chopped green onion
1 1/2 pounds bacon, cooked crisp and crumbled

POTATOES SUPREME: Boil potatoes until tender. Drain well. Add melted butter and half and half to potatoes and coarsely mash. Add cheese, salt and pepper. Season well. Put potatoes in baking dish. Smooth top. Cover with sour cream. Sprinkle generously with green onion and bacon. This may be made the day before and reheated in a 350°F oven for 30-40 minutes.

---

4 large baking potatoes, peeled and cubed
1 stick butter, melted
1/2 cup cream
1/2 cup sour cream
Salt and pepper
1-2 cups sour cream
1 cup grated Gruyère cheese

POTATOES SALIEU: Preheat oven to 350°F. Cook potatoes in salted water until tender, about 20 minutes. Roughly mash potatoes with butter and cream. Add sour cream and season with salt and pepper. Put potatoes in a 6-cup charlotte mold. Pat down firmly. Bake for 30 minutes or until hot. Let cool 5-10 minutes. Unmold potatoes on ovenproof dish, such as a pretty quiche dish. Ice unmolded potatoes with sour cream and top with lots of cheese. Broil until cheese is brown and bubbly.

TO SERVE: Serve immediately.

NOTES: You will notice that Potatoes Salieu have considerably less liquid than Potatoes Supreme. This is what makes them unmold nicely. If they are too soft, they will lose their shape when unmolded. Although these recipes are very similar, one is American and one is French. Green onions and bacon can be added to Potatoes Salieu without changing the basic nature of the dish.

Two Potato and Onion Cake

SERVES 6-8

*I taught this in a holiday menu class. It combines both sweet and
Idaho potatoes. If you do not like sweet potatoes, the dish can be
prepared with only white potatoes. The fun of it, however, is seeing the
different colored layers when cut into rounds. It looks like you spent
hours layering them in a mold, when in fact, it was quite an easy task.*

1/2 cup olive oil

1 sweet potato, peeled and
    thinly sliced

3 Idaho potatoes, peeled and
    thinly sliced

1 yellow onion, sliced

4 large eggs

1 cup heavy cream

1 cup grated Swiss cheese

Salt and pepper

POTATO CAKE: Preheat oven to 400°F. Heat olive oil in
3-quart sauté pan. Sauté potatoes and onions in olive oil
until beginning to soften. Add additional oil if necessary.
Cool. Lightly mix together eggs and cream in large mixing
bowl. Add cheese and cooled potato-onion mixture. Season
with salt and pepper. Pour potato mixture into a 9x13-inch
ovenproof pan. Bake until firm, about 30 minutes.

TO ASSEMBLE AND SERVE: Cut into desired shapes, or use
3-inch round cutter to cut into nice serving size. If you
do not plan to serve potatoes immediately, place rounds
on baking sheet. Reheat in 350°F oven for 10 minutes
or until hot throughout. Rounds should be 1 1/2 to 2
inches high.

*NOTE: This is really a variation on old-fashioned quiche. It
demonstrates that basic skills or recipes can be modernized
and used in a variety of creative ways.*

Potato and Wild Mushroom Napoleons

SERVES 8-10

Potatoes and wild mushrooms are two of my favorite foods, so I devised a special way to present them. After quite a bit of experimenting, I settled on phyllo layers, as they remained crisp, could be made ahead, and even frozen. Then I worked on the filling. When I tried to combine fresh mushrooms with the dried, my potatoes turned black. I settled on seasoning the mixture only with dried mushrooms. Fortunately, the dish turned out well, can be made ahead and reheated, and is attractive on a plate.

---

2 large baking potatoes, peeled
1/2-1 cup milk
1/2 cup cream
Salt and pepper
1 large leek, cleaned
1/2 cup dried mushrooms
1 cup hot water
2-4 tablespoons butter
1/4 cup chopped fresh tarragon
Salt and pepper

FILLING: Cut potatoes into chunks. Cover with salted water. Cook until tender, about 15 minutes. Drain. Add milk, cream, salt, and pepper to potatoes. Purée with hand mixer. Cut leek in half. Wash well. Cut into 1/4-inch dice. Soak dried mushrooms in boiling water for 30 minutes. After 30 minutes, squeeze out excess moisture and chop. Melt butter in small sauté pan. Add mushrooms, leeks, and tarragon. Sauté until leeks are tender and tarragon has released its flavor about 5 minutes. Add leek-mushroom mixture to mashed potatoes. Season. Set aside until ready to use.

Packaged phyllo dough
1 stick butter, melted
1 cup grated white cheese

PHYLLO LAYERS: Preheat oven to 350°F. Cut 4-5 stacked phyllo sheets into 2-inch rounds. Brush one round with melted butter and add a dash of grated cheese. Cover with another round, repeating the layering process 3-4 times. Bake layered rounds for 5 minutes. Allow 3 baked phyllo stacks per person. Watch carefully as these tend to burn easily.

TO ASSEMBLE AND SERVE: Preheat oven to 300°F. Before guests arrive, assemble napoleons. Place one baked phyllo round on baking sheet. Top with 1-2 tablespoons mashed potatoes. Top with another baked phyllo round. Put on another 1-2 tablespoons mashed potatoes. End with third baked phyllo round. Feel free to use only top and bottom of baked phyllo. These are not as high but are easier and still effective. Have potato stacks at room temperature before baking. Bake for 10 minutes or until potatoes are hot.

NOTE: *Mashed potatoes should be stiff enough to stay on phyllo rounds. Do not add too much liquid.*

Rice Mold with Zucchini Band

Although I cooked extensively during my early married life, I was always intimidated by rice. One day I watched a woman who worked for me cook rice. She simply put in more water than rice, a garlic clove and some salt. She brought the water to a boil and then reduced the heat to a simmer. She never covered it. She never stirred. The rice worked every time. So here is easy white rice.

3 cups white rice (Uncle Ben's)
6 cups water or broth
1 tablespoon salt
1 clove garlic

RICE: Put rice and water in saucepan with salt and garlic clove. Stir once or twice. Bring water to boil. Reduce heat to simmer. Do not stir again. Cover or don't cover. Rice will cook faster covered, but it will still be perfect uncovered if you don't stir. Simmer rice about 20 minutes or until all water has evaporated and you can see air holes in rice with no water bubbling up.

TO BAKE RICE: Rice may also be baked in oven. Add 2 cups water for every 1 cup of rice. Cover and put into preheated 350°F oven for 1 hour. You can cook huge amounts in this manner. It can then be reheated in preheated 350°F oven for 20-30 minutes. Reheat, covered, with butter and desired spices.

2 1/2 zucchini, sliced into thin rounds
3 tablespoons butter
1/2 zucchini, seeds removed and diced
1/2 red bell pepper, diced
Rice, seasoned with butter and salt

TO PREPARE MOLD WITH ZUCCHINI BAND: Thinly slice zucchini. (A Feemster is a good device to use for this.) Sauté zucchini for 3-5 minutes in butter. Remove from pan. Reserve. Add diced zucchini and red bell pepper. Sauté 3-5 minutes or until crisp-tender. Add to cooked rice. Add additional butter if necessary.

TO ASSEMBLE: Line individual 6-ounce soufflé dishes with overlapping slices of buttered zucchini. They will stick to sides because of butter. Fill zucchini lined dishes with rice, seasoned with butter, sautéed vegetables, salt and pepper. Pack down. Refrigerate, covered, until ready to serve. May be made a day ahead.

TO SERVE: Reheat rice in preheated 350°F oven for 20 minutes. Turn out onto plate or serving dish.

Baked Four Grain Dressing

SERVES 10-12

This is an interesting recipe because it exposes one to many wonderful types of grains. Feel free to change the variety of rices. Besides great taste, this dish is high in fiber and very healthy. Eliminate the butter and you have a low fat dish. To do this, sauté the vegetables in the chicken broth in which you sautéed the dried mushrooms. This recipe makes quite a lot, so you may want to cut it in half.

1 cup wild rice

2 cups chicken broth

2 ounces dried porcini
   mushrooms

1 stick butter

1 large onion, chopped

2 carrots, diced

1 pound button mushrooms,
   sliced

2 red bell peppers, chopped

2 bay leaves

1 tablespoon thyme

Reserved mushroom soaking
   liquid

1 cup Madeira wine

5 cups chicken or vegetable
   broth

1 cup short grain brown rice
   or Texmati brown rice

1 cup Basmati rice

1 cup kasha

1 cup chopped parsley

Salt and pepper

DRESSING: Cover wild rice with hot water in medium bowl. Let rice soak for at least 30 minutes. Heat 2 cups broth until boiling. Remove from heat. Add porcini mushrooms. Soak mushrooms for 30 minutes or until soft. Chop. Reserve mushrooms and broth. Melt butter in 5-quart sauté pan. Add onion, carrots, button mushrooms, red bell peppers, bay leaf, and thyme. Cover. Cook over moderately low heat, until vegetables are tender, stirring occasionally. This should take about 15 minutes. Add reserved mushroom soaking liquid, Madeira and 5 cups additional chicken broth. Drain wild rice and add along with brown rice, Basmati rice, and kasha. Add parsley. Stir. Bring mixture to boil. Cover. Cook 35 minutes on top of stove or until all moisture has evaporated. Season with salt and pepper. Transfer to baking dish.

TO SERVE: Preheat oven to 350°F. Reheat, covered with a small amount of additional broth for 20-30 minutes. Garnish top with additional parsley.

NOTE: This is a great vegetarian entrée. Vegetables can be varied.

Rice Pilaf

SERVES 8-10

This recipe is especially useful for fall and holiday menus.
It is a good substitute for dressing. I have used it often to fill the
center of a crown of pork.

1/2 stick butter
2 cloves garlic, minced
1 cup chopped onion
1/2 cup chopped red bell
  pepper
3 cups rice (Uncle Ben's)
1/3 cup golden raisins
6 cups chicken broth
2 tablespoons butter
1 pound mushrooms, sliced
2-3 tablespoons minced
  parsley
Salt and pepper

RICE: Melt 1/2 stick butter in 3-quart sauté pan. Add garlic, onion, and red bell pepper. Sauté until tender, about 5-10 minutes. Transfer to mixing bowl. Put rice and raisins in same sauté pan. Add broth. Bring mixture to a boil. Cover. Reduce heat to simmer. Do not stir rice. Cook until rice is done, about 20-30 minutes. You can peek, do not be afraid to lift lid. Melt additional 2 tablespoons butter in small sauté pan. Sauté mushrooms until cooked. Combine bell pepper mixture, rice, and mushrooms. Add parsley. Season with salt and pepper.

TO SERVE: Reheat, covered, in 350°F. oven for 20-30 minutes or reheat on top of stove. If you reheat on top of stove, you may need to add an additional 1/2 cup broth.

NOTE: *Use any combination of rice, for example, Basmati, wild rice or a good brown rice. This is a great recipe for trying new, flavorful rice products.*

Purée of White Beans and Potatoes

SERVES 4-6

White beans and potatoes are both very popular. Combine them to create a doubly good and tasty treat.

1 large potato, peeled and
    cut in large chunks
1 can Great Northern Beans,
    undrained
1/2 cup chicken broth
2-3 tablespoons olive oil
2-3 garlic cloves, minced
1 red bell pepper, chopped
1 teaspoon dried oregano
1 can Great Northern Beans,
    drained and rinsed
1 medium potato, boiled and
    cubed same size as red pepper
Salt and pepper
1/2 teaspoon Tabasco
3 tablespoons chopped parsley

PURÉE: Boil 1 potato, cut in chunks, in water seasoned with salt until very tender, approximately 15-20 minutes. Put boiled potato and 1 can undrained white beans in mixing bowl. Purée together with an electric mixer. Thin purée with chicken broth as needed. Usually 1/2 cup broth is sufficient. Add more if necessary. Heat oil in 3-quart sauté pan. Add garlic, red peppers, and oregano. Sauté over moderately low heat until peppers are tender. Combine puréed potato-white bean mixture with sautéed peppers, 1 drained and rinsed can white beans and the remaining cubed boiled potato. Season with salt and Tabasco. Add parsley for color.

Fresh chopped parsley

TO SERVE: Reheat on top of stove. Put into serving dish. Garnish top with additional parsley.

Vegetables

Fresh Asparagus with Hollandaise   171

Beets with Sour Cream   172

Honey Glazed Carrots   173

Carrot Tart   174

Swiss Chard, Tomato, and Cheese Casserole *   175

Cranberry-Horseradish Mousse   176

Eggplant Stacks with Goat Cheese   177

Garlic Custards   178

Green Beans with Red and Yellow Peppers *   179

Green Beans with Glazed Onions   180

Country Style Green Beans *   181

Leeks au Gratin   182

Piperade (Sautéed Peppers and Scrambled Eggs)   183

Puréed Green Peas   184

Mushroom Strudel with Kale and Red Pepper   185

Red Pepper Timbale   186

Succotash of Lima Beans, Corn and Tomatoes *   187

Great Northern Beans with Zucchini and Carrots   188

— *continued on next page* —

Vegetables

— continued —

Adelaide's Squash   189

Spinach Anne Armstrong or Spinach Timbale with Gorgonzola   190

Creamed Spinach   191

Wild Mushrooms in Puff Pastry Boxes   192

Tomato Tart   193

Green Beans and Wax Beans in Parmesan Cream   194

Zucchini, Red Pepper, and Potato Gratin *   195

Zucchini Timbales with Cumin   196

* denotes a low fat dish

Fresh Asparagus with Hollandaise

SERVES 6-8

*Fresh asparagus is such a good and versatile accompaniment
to so many dinners that I have included this basic recipe.
Serve it cold as a salad, hot with hollandaise or at room
temperature with a vinaigrette.*

---

2 bunches fresh asparagus
1 tablespoon salt

ASPARAGUS: Break off tough ends of asparagus. If they are somewhat tough peel them. Bring large pot of salted water to boil. Drop in asparagus. Cook 3-4 minutes or until crisp-tender. Refresh under ice cold water. Drain on paper towels. Can be done ahead and reheated or served cold.

---

2 egg yolks
Juice of 1 lemon
1/2 teaspoon salt
2 sticks butter, melted and hot

HOLLANDAISE: Place yolks, lemon juice and salt in the food processor. Process to combine. With machine running, begin slowly pouring hot, melted butter through the feed tube. Continue adding butter until mixture is thick.

TO SERVE: Serve asparagus cold with a vinaigrette or hot with hollandaise.

VARIATION: For a large party, cut asparagus into 1-inch to 2-inch pieces. No need to boil; sauté briefly in butter until crisp-tender before serving.

NOTES: Asparagus will not stay green long once you have added vinaigrette. Therefore, add vinaigrette immediately before serving. Asparagus can be cooked as this recipe states the day before serving. To reheat, drop in boiling water for 15-30 seconds. I am always asked if one should peel asparagus. If they are large asparagus, you should peel them. Every fancy restaurant does. For home cooks, it's a matter of time. With limited time, or if you are cooking for a large crowd, buy small, tender asparagus and skip the peeling.

Beets with Sour Cream

*The color of this dish alone should encourage you to try this recipe.
No one will guess they are being served beets. My talented
mother-in-law serves these beets with puréed peas. It is a beautiful
combination at any time, but particularly lovely at Christmas.*

10-12 medium beets
2 cups sour cream
1/2 stick butter, melted
2 teaspoons salt
1 teaspoon pepper

BEETS: Clean beets and boil without the green tops until tender. Do not cut before boiling. Peel and purée cooked beets in food processor with sour cream and butter. Process until smooth. Season with salt and pepper.

TO SERVE: Reheat in 3-quart sauté pan over moderate heat, stirring often. Place in serving dish.

Honey Glazed Carrots

SERVES 4

This recipe produces a beautifully colored, glazed carrot. Use a wide-bottom skillet, as this allows the water, bourbon and honey to coat the surface of each carrot. When combined with green onion, these carrots make a beautiful presentation.

---

1 pound carrots or
  5 cups carrots, peeled and
  sliced on the diagonal,
  1/4-inch thick
2/3 cup water
3 tablespoons butter
3 tablespoons bourbon
3 tablespoons honey
Salt and freshly ground
  pepper
2 tablespoons butter
1 bunch green onions,
  thinly sliced

CARROTS: Place carrots in water in shallow sauté pan. Add butter, bourbon and honey. Cook over medium-high heat until carrots are tender and liquid is reduced to a glaze. This should take about 10-15 minutes. Season with salt and pepper. Melt butter in small sauté pan. Sauté onions until tender, about 3 minutes. Combine green onions with cooked, glazed carrots.

TO SERVE: Reheat carrots in saucepan and transfer to serving plate. You may need to add 1/4 cup water or 2 tablespoons butter to reheat them.

Carrot Tart

SERVES 8

This is one of my oldest teaching tools. I adapted it from a recipe published in Gourmet *many years ago. The color and overall design make it a beautiful side dish.*

---

1 1/4 cups flour
Pinch of salt
1 stick butter, cut into 8
    tablespoons
1/3 cup cold water

(Or, use a Pillsbury ready-made
    pie crust)

DOUGH: Put flour and salt in food processor. Quickly process once. Add butter. Process with on-off motions until butter is the size of "little peas." Once this has happened, turn machine on and pour water through feed tube. When dough is about to form a ball, remove it from machine and form it into a ball with your hands. This dough will be ready to use immediately. Roll out and line a 9-inch flan ring or quiche pan with dough. Bake in 400°F oven until crust is done. Reserve.

---

4 pounds large carrots, peeled
1 tablespoon salt
1 teaspoon sugar
4 tablespoons butter, melted
1/2-3/4 cup sour cream
Salt and pepper
Fresh thyme
2 tablespoons butter

FILLING: Preheat oven to 350°F. Cook carrots in water seasoned with salt and sugar until tender. Cut half the carrots into 1-inch pieces and purée in processor with butter and sour cream. Season with salt and pepper. Place puréed filling into baked pie shell and smooth top. Slice remaining 2 pounds carrots into thin rounds and completely cover top of pie in overlapping circles. Sprinkle with fresh thyme and dot with butter. Refrigerate until ready to serve.

TO SERVE: Bake covered in preheated 350°F oven for 10-15 minutes.

VARIATION: For individual servings, make tarts in small, individual tart shells, 2-3-inches in diameter.

NOTE: If making one large tart, cook large carrots. It will take fewer overlapping slices to cover the surface of the carrot purée. Cook extra carrots to be sure you have enough.

Swiss Chard, Tomato, and Cheese Casserole

SERVES 4-6

*Greens such as swiss chard, kale and turnip greens were once
considered true country fare. Today they have been elevated to
haute cuisine. Here is a recipe that uses greens to create an
interesting recipe that is good for family as well as company.*

---

4 bunches Swiss chard,
   washed and center ribs
   cut away

5 tablespoons olive oil

2 cloves garlic, minced

3 red bell peppers, chopped

1 large onion, chopped

3 large tomatoes, chopped

Salt and pepper

2 cups Monterey Jack cheese,
   grated

1/2 cup Parmesan cheese,
   grated

2 tablespoons additional
   olive oil for top

CASSEROLE: Wash Swiss chard and cut into small pieces
with kitchen shears. (It is safer than cutting chard with
knife.) Heat 3 tablespoons olive oil in 5-quart sauté pan.
Sauté chard in oil, until wilted, about 3 minutes. Stir often.
Transfer chard to colander. Drain, pressing on chard with
back of spoon to release liquid. Heat 2 additional tablespoons oil in same pan. Add garlic, red bell peppers and
onion. Sauté until crisp-tender, about 4 minutes. Add
tomatoes. Tomatoes should be cooked slightly, not well
done or mushy. Remove from heat. Toss to combine red
bell pepper-tomato mixture and chard. Season with salt
and pepper. Place chard mixture in baking dish. Add half
the cheeses to chard mixture. Mix. Sprinkle remaining
cheeses over top. Drizzle with olive oil.

TO SERVE: Preheat oven to 350°F. Bake, uncovered, approximately 15 minutes. If necessary, broil several minutes
for cheeses to brown. Serve immediately.

Cranberry Horseradish Mousse

SERVES 8-10

*Although this is not a vegetable, per se, I included it because it is a
fantastic dish to serve during the holidays or with game.*

1 cup sugar
1/2 cup water
2 cups whole fresh cranberries
1 cup sour cream
4-5 tablespoons prepared
    horseradish
1 tablespoon fresh lemon juice
1 envelope unflavored gelatin
1/2 cup cold water

MOUSSE: Combine sugar and water in saucepan and bring water to a boil. Add berries and cook until popped, about 3-5 minutes. Remove from heat and let cool slightly. Purée berries in processor or blender. Add sour cream, horseradish and lemon juice. Process until mixture is smooth. Combine gelatin and 1/4 cup water in small saucepan and let stand until the gelatin is hard. Place over low heat and stir until gelatin is dissolved completely. (I add another 1/4-cup cold water to dissolve the gelatin.) Liquid should be completely clear. When dissolved, add gelatin to berry mixture and blend thoroughly. Put into a 4-cup mold. Cover with plastic wrap. Refrigerate until set, at least 6 hours or overnight.

TO SERVE: Dip mold in hot water for 10-15 seconds to loosen. Unmold onto serving plate. Decorate platter with fresh herbs and cranberries.

Eggplant Stacks with Goat Cheese

SERVES 6

I think you will find this an unusual, yet wonderful, way to serve eggplant. Each stack is an individual serving, so it looks nice on a plate as well as on a buffet table.

1 eggplant, unpeeled
1 cup unbleached white flour, seasoned with salt and pepper
3 eggs, lightly beaten
1 cup fresh bread crumbs
Olive oil
6 ounces goat cheese, cut into rounds

EGGPLANT: Slice eggplant into 1/4-inch slices. Using a 2-inch round cutter, cut each slice into round shapes. Put seasoned flour, lightly beaten eggs and bread crumbs into three separate bowls. Dip each eggplant round first into flour, then egg, and then bread crumbs. Put small amount of olive oil into skillet. Sauté eggplant rounds on both sides until brown. Put half eggplant rounds onto a baking sheet. Top with 1/2-inch slice of goat cheese. Top with remaining rounds of sautéed eggplant. Reserve until ready to serve. This may be done several hours ahead.

TO SERVE: Heat in preheated 350°F oven until warm, about 10 minutes.

NOTE: *Make your own bread crumbs. The technique is listed in "Before You Begin" on page 2.*

Garlic Custards

SERVES 6

I adapted this recipe from an article in Bon Appétit *almost ten years ago. I have since seen many versions in different books and articles. The flavor is smooth and subtle, not overpowering. I hope you enjoy my version.*

20 cloves garlic, unpeeled,
  or 2 large heads of garlic
1/4 cup olive oil
1 medium pickled jalapeño,
  seeded
3 egg yolks
2 cups heavy cream
2 eggs
Salt and pepper
Cayenne

CUSTARD: Preheat oven to 350°F. Place garlic on a piece of foil. Sprinkle garlic with oil. Close foil tightly. Roast in oven until garlic is very tender, about 30-40 minutes. Reduce temperature to 300°F for baking custards. Cool and extract garlic. Cut off top with kitchen shears. Push garlic purée from bottom into food processor. You should have about 2 tablespoons purée. Mince jalapeño. Add to garlic purée. Add yolks. Process. Add cream, remaining eggs, salt, pepper and cayenne. Process well. Divide mixture among six 3/4-cup ramekins. Place in a baking pan and add about 1/2-inch of hot water (a bain marie). Bake approximately 50 minutes or until a knife inserted in middle comes out clean. Let stand 10 minutes.

1/2 stick melted butter
1/2 cup chopped nuts
1/2 red bell pepper,
  finely chopped
Fresh herbs of choice

TO SERVE: Run a knife around rim of hot ramekins. Unmold onto plate or platter. Sauté nuts, red bell peppers and herbs in melted butter. Pour over tops of unmolded garlic custards.

Green Beans with Red and Yellow Peppers

SERVES 6-8

This is basically a recipe for classic French style green beans. I have added peppers for flavor and color. Substitute sliced, sautéed almonds and, voilà, *you have Green Beans Amandine.*

2-3 pounds Harvester
    green beans
Large pot of salted water
4 tablespoons oil
4 tablespoons butter
3 cloves garlic, chopped
2 yellow bell peppers
2 red bell peppers
Salt and pepper
1 tablespoon dried thyme, or
    2 tablespoons fresh thyme

GREEN BEANS: Break off ends of green beans. Bring large pot of salted water to boil. Add green beans. Cook until crisp tender, about 5-6 minutes. Refresh under ice cold water. Drain and reserve. If refreshed under cold water, these can be done the day before. Put into baggies. They will remain green when reheated. Place oil and butter in deep pot. Add garlic and peppers. Sauté until tender, about 5-10 minutes. When tender, combine peppers and green beans, salt, pepper and thyme.

TO SERVE: Reheat beans and peppers on top of stove. Put into serving dish. Serve hot.

VARIATIONS: *Change thyme to oregano, basil, or a mixture of Italian herbs and you will change the dish. Mix wax beans with green beans for color instead of using peppers.*

NOTES: *Harvesters are wonderful small green beans that we can get locally. Haricots verts (tiny green beans) are hard to find and very expensive but well worth your money. Kentucky Wonders are best cooked country style with bacon and potatoes for a long time.*

Green Beans with Glazed Onions

SERVE 6-8

The balsamic vinegar and Dijon mustard give these green beans
a wonderful and unusual flavor.

2 16-ounce bags pearl onions
1/4 cup balsamic vinegar
2 tablespoons butter
2 tablespoons vegetable oil
2 teaspoons fresh thyme
Salt and pepper
3 pounds fresh green beans
   (Harvesters)
3 tablespoons Dijon mustard
1/4 cup balsamic vinegar
2-4 tablespoons additional
   melted butter

GREEN BEANS: Blanch onions for 1 minute in boiling salted water. Drain and refresh under cold water. Trim root ends and remove the skins. In saucepan, combine vinegar, butter, oil and thyme. Add salt and pepper. Heat until butter is melted. Put onions in baking pan and toss with the butter mixture. Roast in 350°F oven for 35-40 minutes, stirring occasionally, until the onions are brown. Trim green beans and blanch in large pot of boiling water until just tender, about 5 minutes. Drain and refresh under cold water. Return to pot. Add mustard, vinegar and butter. Add onions. Toss together. Season.

TO SERVE: These can be made ahead and reheated in 350°F oven for about 20 minutes.

Country Style Green Beans

SERVES 4-6

This country method of cooking green beans reminds me of my childhood in Nixon, Texas. My grandmother simmered them at least an hour with bacon and potatoes. Pepper was her main seasoning. This method of preparing green beans is the one I use most when cooking for my family. It is a great summer side dish for meats grilled outside.

2 pounds green beans
  (Kentucky Wonders)
3-4 pieces of bacon
  (or 2-3 chunks of salt pork)
1 large potato, peeled and cut
  into large pieces
1/2 onion, chopped
Pepper
Salt to taste

GREEN BEANS: Take ends off green beans, pulling with them any strings that are attached. Wash. Break into 2-inch sections. Put into large pot of salted water. Add bacon, cut into pieces, potatoes and onion. Bring water to a boil. Reduce heat to a simmer. Cook for at least 45 minutes to 1 hour. Pepper well. Add enough salt to give it a good punch.

TO SERVE: Serve green beans in large bowl with bacon, potato and onion. You may drain broth off, but it is so flavorful that I love to serve it along with the green beans.

NOTE: *Make a lot. The beans and broth are even better the next day. Add as many potatoes or onions as you think you can eat. This dish is wonderful served in a bowl with vegetable broth and all three vegetables.*

Leeks au Gratin

SERVES 8-10

I learned to prepare this dish in France at LaVarenne in the late 1970s. The sauce is an excellent base for any vegetable casserole. You will create a dish that can be made the day before serving and that tastes wonderful. Serve this dish with grilled meat or fish that does not have a sauce of its own. This dish can serve as the sauce.

6-8 medium leeks
Salt

LEEKS: Trim leeks, discarding dark green tops. Split leeks lengthwise. Wash thoroughly. Chop them into 1/2-inch thick pieces. Bring large pot of salted water to boil. Add leeks. Cook 8-10 minutes or until tender. Drain. Refresh under cold water. Drain again.

2-3 cups milk
1 slice onion
1 bay leaf
2-3 peppercorns
4 tablespoons butter
4 tablespoons flour
Pinch of nutmeg
Salt and pepper

BÉCHAMEL SAUCE: Heat milk with onion, bay leaf, and peppercorns for 10 minutes to infuse flavors. Reserve. Melt butter in saucepan. Add flour and stir 1-2 minutes or until all flour is incorporated. Add strained milk all at once. Whisk constantly over moderately high heat until mixture is thick. Season with nutmeg, salt, and pepper. If sauce is too thick, thin down with additional milk.

1-2 cups grated Gruyère
   or Swiss cheese

TO ASSEMBLE: Combine leeks and béchamel sauce. Put into baking dish. Top with cheese. Gratin may be prepared up to a day ahead. Keep covered in refrigerator. It can also be frozen.

TO SERVE: Preheat oven to 400°F. Bake gratin for 20-30 minutes or until bubbling hot and cheese is brown. If cheese is not sufficiently brown, broil casserole for several minutes.

VARIATIONS: Substitute toasted bread crumbs for cheese topping. Substitute any vegetable such as squash, broccoli or cauliflower or any combination. Add sautéed mushrooms if desired.

Piperade
(Sautéed Peppers and Scrambled Eggs)

SERVES 8-10

*This is a classic French dish and wonderful for a brunch. The
pepper mixture can be prepared ahead, leaving only the scrambling
of the eggs for the last moment. I have catered this for large crowds,
so I know you will find it useful in your own entertaining.
It is also good for a Sunday night supper with the family.*

---

2 cups ham, cut into
    1/2-inch pieces
2-3 tablespoons olive oil
1 large yellow onion, chopped
1-2 cloves garlic, minced
1 large green bell pepper, cut
    into 1/2-inch pieces
1 large red bell pepper, cut
    into 1/2-inch pieces
3 tomatoes, seeded and cut
    into 1/2-inch pieces
Salt and freshly ground
    black pepper

VEGETABLES: Heat olive oil in a large skillet and brown
ham lightly. Remove from skillet and reserve. In same
skillet, sauté onion, garlic, green and red peppers, and
tomatoes about 10-15 minutes or until onion and peppers
are soft and most of the juice which exudes from the
tomatoes has evaporated. Season with salt and pepper.
(This step may be done ahead.)

4-6 tablespoons butter
1 1/2 dozen eggs, lightly beaten
Salt and freshly ground
    black pepper

EGGS: Heat butter in large skillet. Beat eggs lightly with
salt and pepper. Pour eggs into skillet. Stir until eggs are
scrambled but far from completely cooked. Add reserved
vegetables and ham. Continue to cook until eggs are done
but still creamy. Correct seasoning.

Fresh chopped parsley

TO SERVE: Place on decorative platter and serve immediately.
Garnish with fresh chopped parsley, if desired.

Puréed Green Peas

SERVES 6-8

This is a dish I used often when I was very young. At that time, there was no such thing as a food processor. I would take defrosted, frozen peas and push them through a strainer to remove the shells. It would take hours, but I felt it was well worth the effort because the color is so fantastic. Thanks to the wonderful food processor, puréed peas can now be made in minutes.

4-5 8-ounce boxes frozen
   green peas, defrosted
3/4 stick butter, melted
1 tablespoon each of salt
   and pepper
1/2 teaspoon ground nutmeg

PEAS: Purée peas in several batches in food processor with butter, salt, pepper, and nutmeg. Season with additional salt and pepper if necessary.

Good white sandwich bread
1/2 stick butter, melted

CROUTONS: Cut sandwich bread into 2-3-inch rounds. Using a pastry brush, coat each round with melted butter. Bake in 250°F oven for 1 hour or until crisp and hard.

TO SERVE: Use a large pastry bag fitted with a large rosette tip. Pipe puréed peas decoratively onto an oven proof serving dish, dot with butter and heat in 350°F oven for 10-15 minutes. Another option is to place croutons on baking dish. Pipe puréed peas on top of croutons. Dot with butter. Heat in 350°F oven for 10-15 minutes. Using a spatula, remove individual servings onto a large platter or individual plates. Or, for a simpler presentation, spoon hot peas into serving dish and serve.

Mushroom Strudel with Kale and Red Pepper

SERVES 6-8

*Phyllo pastry is easy to work with and has innumerable uses.
In this recipe, it is used to encase sautéed vegetables. It can be
prepared the day before serving, or frozen and defrosted in the
refrigerator before baking. It is a glamorous way to serve
any combination of vegetables.*

1 bunch kale, tough stems
   removed
4 tablespoons butter
2 cloves garlic, minced
1 red bell pepper, chopped
1 pound mushrooms, sliced
Juice of one lemon
1 teaspoon dried thyme
Salt and pepper
4 tablespoons flour
1/2 cup chicken broth
1/4 cup freshly grated
   Parmesan cheese
Salt and pepper

VEGETABLE FILLING: Remove tough stems running down middle of kale. Wash kale well. Cut into small pieces with kitchen shears. Bring a large pot of salted water to a boil. Boil kale until tender, about 10 minutes. Drain well, pressing out all excess moisture with the back of a spoon or squeeze out excess moisture with your hands. Reserve. Melt butter in 3-quart sauté pan. Add garlic, red pepper and mushrooms. Season with lemon juice, dried thyme, salt and pepper. Sauté over moderate heat until tender. Once vegetables are tender, add flour. Stir until no traces of flour appear. Cook 1-2 minutes. Add kale. Add 1/2 cup chicken broth. Cook, stirring constantly until mixture is very thick. You want this to bind vegetables together. Add Parmesan cheese. Season with salt and pepper. Cool.

3/4 stick butter, melted and
   cooled
4 sheets of phyllo dough
1/3 cup Parmesan cheese

STRUDEL: Melt butter in small saucepan. Place 1 phyllo sheet on baking pan with sides. Brush lightly with melted butter. Sprinkle with Parmesan cheese. Top with another sheet of phyllo. Brush again with melted butter and Parmesan. Repeat this with 2 additional pastry sheets, laying each sheet on top of the other. Place cooled vegetable filling in the middle of the phyllo sheets. Tuck sheets around vegetable mixture, forming a loaf. Sprinkle with additional Parmesan cheese. If not serving immediately, cover and place in refrigerator.

TO SERVE: Preheat oven to 350°F. Bake strudel 30 minutes, or until pastry is a golden brown. Transfer to serving platter. Slice to serve.

NOTE: Use muffin tins to make individual strudels. Tear one piece of phyllo into a 4-inch piece. Butter and sprinkle with Parmesan cheese and place in muffin tin. Repeat this 3-4 times. Put in a large tablespoon of vegetable filling. Fold phyllo over filling. Bake until golden brown.

Red Pepper Timbale

SERVES 6

*This is a colorful dish with a soothing, delightful flavor. It would be
a good accompaniment for any entrée—meat, fish or chicken.*

4 red bell peppers
3 egg yolks
2 whole eggs
1 teaspoon salt
1/2 teaspoon pepper
1/4 cup Parmesan cheese
1 cup half and half or
   heavy cream

TIMBALE: Char red peppers under broiler on all sides. Cool in tea towel. Peel and seed peppers. Slice two of the peppers into 1/4 inch strips. Reserve. Place remaining two peppers into food processor. Add egg yolks, eggs, salt, pepper and cheese to peppers and process until smooth. With machine on, pour cream through feed tube. Preheat oven to 350°F. Coat six 6-ounce timbale molds or soufflé dishes with a non-stick cooking spray. Place filled dishes in a pan of hot water (bain marie). Bake until set, about 30 minutes. Custards will be puffed slightly and firm to the touch when done.

2-3 tablespoons butter
Reserved red bell pepper slices
1/4 cup chopped chives
Salt and freshly ground
   black pepper

TO SERVE: Melt butter in small skillet. Add reserved sliced red peppers and chives. Heat. Season with salt and freshly ground pepper. Let custards cool 10 minutes. Run a knife around custard cups. Unmold onto serving platter or individual plates. Top each mold with red pepper-chive mixture.

NOTE: If you choose to bake this in one large soufflé dish, increase cooking time to 45 minutes-1hour.

Succotash of Lima Beans, Corn, and Tomatoes

SERVES 6-8

My love for this recipe reveals my country roots. Lima beans, corn and fresh tomatoes are all good, basic vegetables.

1/4 cup olive oil

1/2 large onion, chopped

2-3 cloves garlic, chopped

1 1-pound bag frozen *baby* lima beans, defrosted

4 cups chicken broth

1 8-ounce box frozen corn, defrosted

1 large tomato, chopped

Salt and pepper

1-2 tablespoons cumin

3 tablespoons sour cream or light sour cream

SUCCOTASH: Heat oil in 3-quart sauté pan. Add onion and garlic. Cook over moderately low heat for 3-5 minutes, or until vegetables are soft. Add lima beans, broth, corn and tomato. Season with salt, pepper, and cumin. Add sour cream. Cook over moderately low heat for 1 hour. The secret to making frozen lima beans tender is cooking them a long time. Juice will become thicker the longer they cook.

VARIATION: *Omit cumin and substitute fresh basil or dried thyme.*

NOTE: *If you use cumin, add enough to taste it. Just decide how much you like.*

Great Northern Beans with Zucchini and Carrots

Serves 10-12

This dish is especially valuable for the busy cook. It uses canned white beans and can be put together in several minutes. Use your imagination to enhance the beans. The options are unlimited.

1/3 cup chicken broth
2 cloves garlic, chopped
1/2 cup chopped onion
3 cans Bush's Great Northern Beans
3 cups chicken broth
1 cup heavy cream
2 teaspoons minced fresh rosemary
Salt and pepper

BEANS: Place 1/3 cup chicken broth in 3-quart sauté pan. Add garlic and onion and sauté until tender, about 3-5 minutes. Wash and drain beans. Add beans, 3 cups broth, cream and rosemary to sauté pan with garlic and onion. Cook 45 minutes over moderately low heat until liquid becomes thick. Season with salt and pepper.

2 tablespoons butter
2-3 small zucchini, thinly sliced
2 cups thinly sliced small carrots
Water with teaspoon of sugar

TO ENHANCE DISH: Melt butter in sauté pan. Add zucchini. Sauté until crisp-tender. Bring a sauce pan of water seasoned with sugar to boil. Parboil carrots for 2-3 minutes. Drain.

TO SERVE: Combine zucchini, carrots, and beans. Heat and pour into serving dish.

VARIATIONS: Wash fresh spinach and add to beans right before serving or add sautéed red bell pepper or any vegetable of your choice. Replacing rosemary with oregano, thyme, tarragon, or sage will yield a new taste.

Adelaide's Squash

SERVES 6-8

This recipe demonstrates my love for simple country fare. Fresh squash and fresh tomatoes could possibly come from a garden. Bacon is a must for flavor. For a moment, forget cholesterol and enjoy this good country casserole.

4 yellow squash, sliced
2 zucchini, sliced
3/4 stick butter
2 cups chopped tomatoes
1 onion, chopped
1 cup heavy cream
Salt and pepper
1 cup grated Swiss cheese
6 slices bacon, cooked crisp
   and crumbled

SQUASH: Slice squash and zucchini into 1/4-inch rounds. Place in a 3-quart sauté pan with enough salted water to barely cover vegetables. Bring water to a boil. Boil squash for 3-5 minutes, or until crisp-tender. Drain. Melt butter in a 3-quart sauté pan. Add tomatoes and onion and sauté until tender. Once tender, add cooked squash. Add cream and reduce over high heat until mixture begins to thicken. Season to taste. Put into baking dish and sprinkle with cheese and bacon.

TO SERVE: Bake in 350°F oven until hot and bubbling. Dish can be made the day before serving. Reheat and serve directly from baking dish.

Spinach Anne Armstrong

SERVES 6-8

Spinach Timbale with Gorgonzola

SERVES 10-12

Spinach Anne Armstrong became a staple in my home 20 years ago because my children adored it. I came across Spinach Timbale with Gorgonzola in Bon Appétit. *It used all the ingredients in Spinach Anne Armstrong and dressed up my old favorite. Bake the new version in individual timbale molds. It is foolproof and looks great on a plate. It is attractive in the center of a plate with meat such as lamb, pork, or beef stacked against it. I chose this dish to be the focal point of the front cover.*

2 8-ounce packages frozen chopped spinach, defrosted
1 16-ounce carton cottage cheese
2 cups American cheese
1 tablespoon flour
1 egg
2 tablespoons butter, melted
Salt and pepper to taste

SPINACH ANNE ARMSTRONG: Preheat oven to 350°F. Squeeze out excess moisture from spinach. Do this with your hands or in a tea towel. Combine all remaining ingredients and put into an ovenproof dish.

TO SERVE: Bake for 30 minutes or until cheeses are bubbling. Serve hot from baking dish.

3 8-ounce packages frozen chopped spinach, defrosted with no moisture taken out
24 ounces cottage cheese
4 ounces Gorgonzola, finely crumbled
2 tablespoons butter, melted
5 large eggs
3 tablespoons flour
Salt and pepper to taste

SPINACH TIMBALE WITH GORGONZOLA: Preheat oven to 350°F. Put all ingredients into mixing bowl and mix well. Coat individual 6-ounce timbale molds with non-stick cooking spray and fill them 3/4 full with spinach mixture. Bake in water bath (bain marie) for 45 minutes or until firm and slightly puffed. Let sit 10 minutes before serving.

TO SERVE: Run knife around outside edges of molds. Turn out onto desired plate or platter.

NOTES: Be sure to crumble Gorgonzola finely or one mold will have a big chunk and another will have nothing. Change the cheese in either dish and change its character. You must use frozen, chopped spinach. Frozen whole spinach cannot be adequately chopped in food processor or with a knife.

Creamed Spinach

SERVES 10-12

This is an easy recipe that you will use often. I guarantee that it will be one of the most popular items you serve. It is especially valuable because it can be prepared easily for large crowds.

9 8-ounce packages frozen
    chopped spinach, defrosted
1 stick butter, melted
1 quart half and half cream
Juice of 1/2 lemon per three
    packages of spinach
Salt and pepper
1/2 teaspoon nutmeg per 3
    packages of spinach

SPINACH: Squeeze out all excess moisture from defrosted spinach by putting 1 package at a time in a tea towel and extracting moisture with your hands. Place 3 packages of dry spinach in food processor at one time. Add 1/3 stick melted butter and 1 cup half and half. Add lemon juice, salt, pepper, and nutmeg. Add at least 1 teaspoon salt. Process until smooth. Add additional cream if necessary to achieve smooth, light purée. You do not want excess cream. Add only as much cream as spinach will absorb. Repeat until all spinach is puréed. Correct seasoning.

TO SERVE: Heat on top of stove, over moderately low heat until hot, stirring often. Place in an attractive serving dish.

NOTE: Spinach can be prepared the day before serving. Reheat on top of the stove or, covered, in a preheated 300°F oven for 20-30 minutes.

Wild Mushrooms in Puff Pastry Boxes

SERVES 8

The idea for this elegant side dish came from a professional cooking
publication. It can be prepared easily with frozen puff pastry.
Use it as a main course by adding meat to filling.

2 10-inch square sheets frozen
    puff pastry
Egg glaze (1 egg mixed with
    1 tablespoon water)

PUFF PASTRY BOXES: Preheat oven to 375°F. On a lightly floured work surface, lay one sheet of puff pastry. Roll it out slightly and cut it into nine 3-inch squares. Place squares of puff pastry on baking sheet. With a fork, punch several holes into squares. Brush with egg glaze. Slightly roll out the other puff pastry sheet and cut into identical sized squares. Place these squares on top of prepared puff pastry on baking sheet. Using small sharp knife, cut an outline inside top square leaving a 1-inch border. Do not cut through to bottom square. Brush center with egg glaze. Decorate with pastry leaves, hearts, etc., if you desire. Bake until puffy and golden and cut section is bursting out, about 15-20 minutes. Remove from oven and allow to cool on racks. Remove center cutouts, or "lids," with tip of sharp knife. Set aside. Boxes can be frozen at this point.

2-3 tablespoons dried wild
    mushrooms
1 cup hot water
2 tablespoons olive oil
4 cups assorted fresh wild
    mushrooms, sliced
1/3 cup chopped green onion
2-3 cloves garlic, minced
2 tablespoons butter
2 tablespoons flour
1 cup beef broth
1 cup water used in rehydrating
    dried mushrooms
1 tablespoon Bovril
1/3 cup chopped chives
Salt and pepper to taste
Chives, whole

FILLING: Place dried wild mushrooms in 1 cup of boiling hot water. Allow to sit 20-30 minutes or until soft. Chop and reserve mushrooms and water. Strain water through sieve lined with cheesecloth to remove all grit. Heat olive oil in 3-quart sauté pan. Add mushrooms, onion and garlic and sauté for 5 minutes or until mushrooms are tender. Add butter and heat until it is melted. Stir in flour and cook 1-2 minutes. Pour in broth and reserved water from rehydrated dried mushrooms. Stir over high heat until mixture is thick and smooth. Add Bovril and chopped chives. Season with salt and pepper

TO ASSEMBLE AND SERVE: Reheat pastry boxes in 350°F oven for 10 minutes. Fill bottom half with mushroom mixture. Stick several whole chives out one side. Top with top section of puff pastry.

VARIATION: Turn boxes into a dessert. Before baking, brush bottom squares with a good jelly and some sugar. Top with second square. Sprinkle with sugar. Bake as in recipe. Fill with custard, berries, ice cream or fresh fruit.

Tomato Tart

SERVES 6-8

The inspiration for this dish came from George Blanc. It is one of the prettiest dishes in this book. Creating this tart will make you feel like an authentic French chef.

Pillsbury pie crust

DOUGH: Fit pie crust in a 10-inch quiche pan. Put another glass 9-inch pie plate on top or use pie weights. Bake shell in preheated 400°F oven until brown, about 20-30 minutes. Remove from oven. Cool. Remove glass pie plate.

1/4 cup olive oil
1 cup chopped onion
2 garlic cloves, chopped
1 tablespoon tomato paste
1 28-ounce cans tomatoes,
  drained and chopped
Salt and pepper
1/2 teaspoon powdered
  saffron
1 bay leaf
1 tablespoon thyme
1/4 cup chopped parsley
2 red bell peppers, roasted
  and peeled
12 large black olives, pitted

FILLING: Heat olive oil in 3-quart sauté pan. Sauté onions in olive oil until golden. Add garlic, tomato paste and tomatoes. Season with salt and pepper. Add saffron, bay leaf, thyme and parsley. Cook, stirring frequently, until most of liquid has evaporated. This will take 30-40 minutes. Char red bell peppers under a broiler on all sides. Place in a bowl. Cover with plastic wrap until cool enough to handle. Peel red bell peppers and cut into long strips. Cut olives in half. Preheat oven to 400°F. Spread tomato mixture evenly over baked pie shell. Arrange red bell pepper strips on top of tomato mixture to form a lattice pattern. Place 1/2 olive, cut side down, in center of each lattice diamond. Brush surface lightly with olive oil to make it shine.

TO SERVE: Heat tart in 350°F oven for 10-15 minutes, or until hot. Do not forget to brush top of tart with olive oil; it will make it shine. This small trick elevates the tart from good looking to spectacular!

Green Beans and Wax Beans in Parmesan Cream

SERVES 4-6

*Wax beans do not have strings attached and are, therefore, easy to
clean. Just break off the ends. They are tender and colorful. When
wax beans are not in season, substitute sliced yellow bell peppers.*

---

2 pounds mixed small green
  beans (Harvesters) and
  wax beans, ends removed
4 tablespoons butter
3/4 cup cream
Juice of 1 lemon
Salt and pepper

BEANS: Bring large pot of salted water to boil. When
water is boiling, add both types of beans and cook until
crisp-tender, about 3-5 minutes. Snap into 2-inch pieces
before cooking, if desired. (Hopefully, you will find some
Harvester beans. The use of large green beans will keep
this dish from being special.) In large skillet, melt butter.
Add beans, cream and lemon juice. Season with salt and
pepper. Reduce cream until thick and beans are coated.

1/3 cup freshly grated
  Parmesan cheese

TO SERVE: Reheat beans in skillet and toss with Parmesan
cheese. Serve immediately.

NOTE: *Do not add the cheese until you are ready to serve
the beans.*

Zucchini, Red Pepper, and Potato Gratin

SERVES 8

This is a master recipe that will serve you well, not only because it is good company fare, but because it is easy enough to prepare often for your family. The fun is making this exact recipe once and then changing it. Here is your chance to become a truly creative cook.

....

1/2 cup olive oil
6 cloves garlic, chopped
3 large potatoes, peeled, sliced
 into 1/2-inch rounds
4 zucchini, sliced into
 1/4-inch rounds
2 red bell peppers, sliced
 into 1/2-inch strips
2 teaspoons dried thyme or
 4 teaspoons fresh thyme
Salt and pepper

GRATIN: Use some of the olive oil to lightly coat a deep 8-10 cup casserole. Place 2 cloves of chopped garlic in bottom. Place layer of potatoes on top of garlic. Add layer of zucchini, then layer of red bell pepper. Top each layer with chopped garlic, additional olive oil and some thyme. Salt and pepper each layer.

....

TO SERVE: Preheat oven to 375°F. Cover casserole with foil or lid. Bake for 1 1/2 hours. Serve in casserole dish.

VARIATION: *Use oregano, rosemary or any combination of herbs. Add tomatoes, yellow squash, yellow bell peppers, or any vegetable that produces moisture when cooked.*

NOTE: *Do not substitute green beans as they will not cook well in gratin.*

Zucchini Timbales with Cumin

SERVES 8

Cumin gives this recipe its unique character. Once cooked, the zucchini may be put into small molds, reheated and unmolded before serving. Or for a more casual affair, it can be served on one large platter.

8-10 large zucchini
1 tablespoon salt
1 stick butter
4 cloves garlic, chopped
3/4 cup chopped green onion
2-3 tablespoons ground cumin
Salt and pepper

ZUCCHINI: Wash zucchini. It does not need to be peeled. Shred zucchini with shredding blade of food processor. Place shredded zucchini in colander and sprinkle with salt. Let sit for 30 minutes or longer. Place zucchini in a tea towel and squeeze out excess moisture. Melt butter in 3-quart sauté pan. Add garlic and onion. Sauté over moderately high heat until soft, about 3-5 minutes. Add zucchini and seasonings. Sauté until zucchini is barely tender, about 2-3 minutes. Pack zucchini into individual 6-ounce ramekins or timbale molds and cover with foil. Refrigerate until ready to serve.

TO SERVE: Preheat oven to 350°F. Bake for 20 minutes or until hot. Unmold onto serving plate. There is no trick to getting them out. Give them a sharp rap if necessary and they will come right out.

Desserts

Old Fashioned Apple Pie with Cranberries   199

Free Form Apple Tart   200

Banana Napoleons   201
Caramel Sauce

Frozen Blackberry and White Chocolate Mousse   202
Blackberry Sauce

Oreo Cheesecake   203
Chocolate Sauce

Glamorous Chocolate Mousse Cake   204

Chocolate Soufflé with Chocolate Surprise   205
Vanilla Cream Sauce

Cream Cheese Crêpes   207
Apricot Sauce

Classic Crème Brûlée   208

Floating Island   209

French Lace Cookie Tacos   210
Mango Sauce *

Strawberry Sorbet *   211

Lemon Curd Base   212
Lemon Curd Dessert Sauce

— continued on next page —

Desserts

— continued —

Cornucopias with Lemon Cream   213
Raspberry Sauce *

Lemon Custard Tart   214

Frozen Lemon Tower with Fresh Fruit   215

Tiny Tarts with Lemon Curd   216

Fresh Lime Pie   217

Macadamia Nut Pie   218

Adelaide's Peach Cobbler   219

Pear Tart   220

Kathryn's Pecan Pie   221

Strawberry Ice Peppers *   222
Mango Sauce *

denotes a low fat dish

Old Fashioned Apple Pie with Cranberries

SERVES 8-10

*Make your own pastry dough as sheets of prepared pastry are not
big enough to cover the top of this pie. I also decorate the top with a
pastry rose and leaves. I learned this glamorous trick from
Jack Lirio, who teaches cooking in San Francisco.*

---

2 1/2 cups flour
1/2 teaspoon salt
12 tablespoons butter, cut
    into 12 pieces
4 tablespoons Crisco, cold
2/3 cup cold water

DOUGH: Place flour and salt in food processor. Process to combine. Add butter and Crisco. Process in pulses until fats resemble "little peas". With machine running, pour water through feed tube. Immediately before dough forms a ball, turn machine off. Remove dough from processor. Form into a ball with your hands. You may refrigerate or freeze dough until ready to use; however, it should be ready to use immediately. If dough is too soft, refrigerate for 30 minutes. Divide dough in half. Roll one half out on a floured pastry cloth. Press into a 10-inch pie plate. Let dough hang over sides.

10-12 Golden Delicious apples
    or similar good baking apples
1-2 cups sugar
2 tablespoons cornstarch
2 teaspoons cinnamon
1/4 teaspoon nutmeg
1 cup raw cranberries
Juice of 1 or 2 lemons

FILLING: Peel and core apples. Slice into 1/2-inch slices. Combine with sugar, cornstarch, cinnamon, nutmeg and cranberries. Sprinkle lemon juice over all. (Cranberries are not essential, but they add color and taste.)

Pastry dough
Apple filling
Egg glaze (1 egg beaten with
    1 tablespoon water)

TO FINISH DISH: Pile apple mixture into pie shell. Mound as high as possible, about 3-4 inches above rim of pie shell. Roll out remaining half of dough. Brush bottom rim of dough with egg glaze. Place rolled out dough over filling. Tuck pastry down into sides of pie. Use left over dough to decorate top. Make 4 slits in top crust.

TO BAKE: Preheat oven to 450°F. Bake pie 15 minutes or until crust is brown. Turn heat down to 350°F. Continue to bake pie another 20-30 minutes or until apples are tender. To test apples for tenderness, stick a fork through slits in pastry.

TO SERVE: Serve hot, warm, or room temperature.

Free Form Apple Tart

SERVES 6-8

*This is such a simple yet delicious recipe that I had to include it.
You may use a Pillsbury ready made pastry sheet but, since it is so
simple, I would suggest making your own pastry. It is a wonderful
dessert year around. Apples tend to say "fall," but the lightness of
the dessert also says "summer picnic."*

1 1/4 cup white flour
Dash of salt
3/4 stick butter, cut into
　tablespoons
2 tablespoons Crisco
1/3 cup cold water

PASTRY: Put flour and salt in food processor fitted with
steel blade. Add butter and Crisco, cut into tablespoons.
Process with on-off turns until fats resemble "little peas".
Turn machine on and pour in water through feed tube.
Immediately before pastry forms a ball, turn machine off
and form into a ball with your hands. Refrigerate if dough
is too soft, but dough should be usable immediately.

4-5 Delicious or Granny
　Smith apples, peeled and
　cut into thin slices
1/4 cup granulated sugar
1-2 tablespoons butter

TO ASSEMBLE TART: Roll out dough on pastry cloth. Cut
into a 10-inch round. Turn up edges to form a lip on the
pastry. Pierce bottom all over with a fork. Peel, core, and
thinly slice apples. Beginning at the outer edge, arrange
slices in an overlapping design all pointing in the same
direction. Overlap the next row in the other direction.
Continue alternating the direction of the rows until you
have covered the entire surface of the tart. Sprinkle with
granulated sugar. Dot with butter.

1/3 cup apple jelly
2 tablespoons water

TO SERVE: Preheat oven to 400°F. Bake tart for 25-30
minutes. Melt apple jelly with water in small saucepan.
Remove tart from oven and cool slightly. Brush jelly
glaze on top of apple slices. Cut into slices and serve.

VARIATIONS: *Using a small strainer, sprinkle confectioners'
sugar around the outer edges if you desire. You may
sprinkle with toasted, sliced almonds. Change this simple tart
by changing the fruit. What fun to make all kinds and lay
them out on your buffet table or picnic cloth!*

Banana Napoleons
Caramel Sauce

SERVES 8

The idea for this recipe came from a dessert served at the Magnolia Grill in Durham, N.C. A friend in Houston gave me the caramel sauce recipe. It is amazingly simple and absolutely fabulous.

Frozen puff pastry
Egg glaze (1 egg beaten with
  1 tablespoon water)

PASTRY: Preheat oven to 400°F. Defrost two sheets of frozen puff pastry in refrigerator overnight. Roll dough only slightly. Cut sheets into rounds with 2-inch round pastry cutter. Coat top of each round with egg glaze before decorating. Decorate top of each round with small pastry leaves or design of your choice. Bake for 20-30 minutes or until puffed and golden. Split pastry to make a top and bottom. These can be frozen at this point. Reheat 10 minutes in 400°F oven before using.

2 cups milk
1/2 vanilla bean, split
1 teaspoon vanilla
6 egg yolks
2/3 cup sugar
4 tablespoons cornstarch

FILLING: Place milk, vanilla bean, and vanilla in saucepan and bring to boil. Remove vanilla bean. With an electric mixer, beat egg yolks with sugar until mixture turns pale yellow and is very thick. Gently stir in cornstarch. Gradually pour hot milk into egg yolk mixture, stirring constantly. When fully incorporated, pour mixture back into saucepan. Boil for 1 minute, whisking constantly, or until very thick. Cool. Cover surface with plastic wrap until ready to use. Refrigerate. This may be done several days ahead.

1 cup butter
1 pound light brown sugar
3/4 cup Karo syrup, white
1 14-ounce can condensed
  milk (Eagle Brand)
1/2 teaspoon salt
1 teaspoon lemon juice
1/2 cup half and half
1 teaspoon vanilla

CARAMEL SAUCE: Put all ingredients in double boiler and cook over low heat for 1 1/2 hours.

1 cup heavy cream
3-4 bananas

TO SERVE: Whip cream until soft peaks form. Mix into vanilla cream. Add sliced bananas. Place bottom pastry layer on plate. Spoon on bananas and cream. Top with decorated layer. Pour caramel sauce around Napoleons.

Frozen Blackberry and White Chocolate Mousse
Blackberry Sauce

Serves 8-10

This is a particularly valuable recipe because it can be prepared several days before serving. Any frozen berry may be used.

1 16-ounce package frozen blackberries, defrosted
1/2 cup sugar
2 tablespoons cassis, kirsch or any berry liqueur
1 tablespoon lemon juice
6-7 ounces white chocolate (white chocolate with nuts is optional)
2 tablespoons vanilla
3/4 cup sugar
1/4 cup water
6 large egg yolks
3 cups heavy cream

MOUSSE: Purée one 16-ounce package of berries with sugar in food processor until smooth. Place in a saucepan. Add 2 tablespoons liqueur. Heat mixture until sugar has melted. Turn heat to moderately high and reduce mixture to 1 cup. Add lemon juice. Remove to mixing bowl. Cool. Melt white chocolate over low heat in a double boiler. This will take only a few minutes. Cool slightly. Add vanilla. Combine sugar, water, and egg yolks in clean double boiler. Heat until mixture is thick, stirring constantly. Add white chocolate mixture. In another bowl, whip cream until stiff peaks form. Fold all of white chocolate mixture into whipped cream. Line a loaf pan with plastic wrap. Place 1/3 mixture into loaf pan. Mix another 1/3 white chocolate mixture with berry purée. Place mixture on top of plain white chocolate mixture. Top berry mixture with the remaining 1/3 plain white chocolate mixture. Freeze.

1 16-ounce package frozen blackberries, defrosted
1/4 cup sugar
2 tablespoons cassis, kirsch or any berry liqueur

BLACKBERRY SAUCE: Purée remaining 16-ounce package of blackberries with sugar in small saucepan. Add cassis or kirsch or another berry liqueur. Heat over low heat until sugar has melted. Add additional sugar if you think berries should be sweeter. Strain. Cool.

Fresh berries
Fresh mint leaves

TO SERVE: Remove mousse from pan, slice, and place on individual plates. Using a fork, drizzle sauce on top. Arrange fresh berries randomly on plates. Use a variety of colored berries to make the dish more colorful. Garnish with an edible green leaf, such as mint, if desired.

Oreo Cheesecake

SERVES 10-12

This unique cheesecake will especially delight chocolate lovers.
I have served it at fancy dinner parties as well as at a graduation
party for my daughter. It freezes well, allowing you to make
it in advance for large groups. To be really decadent, serve
it with chocolate sauce.

3-4 cups graham cracker crumbs
1 stick butter, melted
1/2 cup firmly packed light brown sugar
1 teaspoon cinnamon

GRAHAM CRACKER CRUST: Purée graham crackers in processor, or buy box of crumbs already made. Mix crumbs with butter, sugar and cinnamon. Press crust onto bottom of 10-inch springform pan. Refrigerate crust until firm, about 30 minutes.

2 pounds cream cheese
1 1/4 cups sugar
2 tablespoons flour
4 extra large eggs
2 egg yolks
1/3 cup whipping cream
1 teaspoon vanilla
1 1/2 cups Oreo cookies, coarsely chopped

FILLING: Preheat oven to 425°F. Beat cream cheese with an electric mixer until smooth. Beat in sugar and flour. Add eggs, yolks, cream, and vanilla. Mix well and pour half of batter into prepared crust. Sprinkle with chopped Oreos. Pour remaining batter over Oreos, smoothing with spatula. Bake cake for 15 minutes. Reduce oven temperature to 225°F. Bake an additional 50 minutes, covering top loosely with foil if browning too quickly.

8 ounces semi-sweet chocolate
1/2 cup heavy cream

GLAZE: Combine chocolate and cream in double boiler. Heat until mixture is smooth.

1 pound semi-sweet chocolate
1 cup heavy cream
1 teaspoon vanilla

CHOCOLATE SAUCE: Mince chocolate into tiny pieces, or use semi-sweet chocolate chips. Melt in double boiler with cream and vanilla.

TO SERVE: Remove cake from springform pan to platter. Pour glaze over top and let it run freely down sides. Refrigerate until ready to serve or freeze. Defrost overnight in refrigerator if frozen. Slice to serve. Using a fork, "throw" chocolate sauce decoratively on top of each slice.

Glamorous Chocolate Mousse Cake

SERVES 12-14

*Ann Marie Huste in New York taught me a variation of this recipe
in my very first cooking school in 1976. One ingredient in this dessert
was a cookie called Cat's Tongue by Fedora. I can no longer find
them, so I substitute Keebler's Deluxe Grahams. This beautiful
dessert can be frozen up to one week before serving.*

1 package Keebler's Deluxe
   Grahams cookies
1/4 stick butter (optional)

CRUST: Cut circle of wax paper to fit bottom of 10-inch spring form pan. You can buy precut parchment rounds that should fit perfectly. Spray paper with non-stick cooking spray. This will help it adhere to bottom of pan. Line side of mold with Deluxe Grahams. If cookies don't stick, place a speck of butter in middle of each cookie. Line side of mold with cookies, flat side facing out. Have cookies touching each other. (You will have some left over.)

1 1/4 pounds semi-sweet
   chocolate chips
1/2 cup white rum
1/2 cup heavy cream
1 tablespoon vanilla
1/4 cup confectioners' sugar
1/2 cup finely ground almonds
1 1/2 sticks butter, softened
3 cups heavy cream
6 tablespoons confectioners'
   sugar

MOUSSE: Melt chocolate in top of double boiler with rum and 1/2 cup cream. This will happen fairly quickly, so watch it closely. Add vanilla. Cool. Combine 1/4 cup confectioners' sugar and almonds. Process in food processor until finely ground. With machine running, drop butter through feed tube, one tablespoon at a time. Process until mixture is smooth. Fold butter-almond mixture into melted chocolate mixture. Whip 3 cups heavy cream until cream forms soft peaks and is thickened. At this time, begin adding the 6 tablespoons confectioners' sugar. Continue to whip cream until stiff peaks form. Fold whipped cream into chocolate mixture, reserving 1/2 cup for decoration. Pour finished chocolate mixture into prepared pan. Cover with plastic wrap and freeze until ready to use.

1/4 cup cocoa powder
Reserved whipped cream

TO SERVE: Turn mold upside down onto flat serving platter. Open ring mold and it will come off perfectly. Remove bottom and paper. Using small strainer, sprinkle cocoa powder all over top. Fit pastry bag with rosette tip and fill bag with reserved whipped cream. Pipe rosettes of whipped cream around edges of top. Tie 1-2 ribbons together into a bow around cake, covering butter if used. Place in freezer until ready to serve. Serve directly from the freezer or you may refrigerate it overnight and serve it as a softer mousse cake. Add fresh flowers to bow for glamorous effect.

Chocolate Soufflé with Chocolate Surprise Vanilla Cream Sauce

SERVES 8

I became acquainted with this dessert in Europe in the early '90s. It is a very practical dessert because it can be done ahead and frozen. The soufflés are even baked frozen so there is no work the day of your party. You will find that this dish has an amazing impact on guests. They are served a simple soufflé only to be surprised by the rich, creamy chocolate center. Such dishes make me think cooking is magical.

---

8 ovenproof ramekins, about 3 1/2-inches in diameter or with 6-ounce capacity
Parchment paper

MOLDS: Line bottoms of each ramekin with rounds of parchment paper. Spray bottom and sides of molds with non-stick cooking spray. Spray parchment to help it adhere to bottom of molds.

1/2 cup heavy cream
6 ounces semi-sweet chocolate

CHOCOLATE SURPRISE: Put cream and chocolate in double boiler. Melt chocolate and cream, stirring occasionally until well combined and no traces of cream appear. Line a loaf pan with plastic wrap. Pour in melted chocolate mixture. The pan should be small enough to yield a 1-inch thick layer of chocolate. Refrigerate until chocolate is hard, 3-4 hours or overnight. When chocolate is firm, use a 1-inch round cutter to cut chocolate sheet into round plugs. You can use your hands to form them if you desire. They will be slightly soft if you handle them, so refrigerate them again while preparing soufflé.

---

10 ounces semi-sweet chocolate
12 tablespoons unsalted butter
6 eggs, separated
1 1/4 cups confectioners' sugar
1 3/4 cups flour
Reserved egg whites

CHOCOLATE SOUFFLÉ: Melt chocolate and butter over moderately low heat in top of double boiler. Cool to room temperature. In mixer, beat egg yolks and sugar until mixture is pale and triples in volume. Fold cooled melted chocolate into yolk-sugar mixture. Carefully fold in flour. Batter will be very thick after the addition of flour. Beat reserved egg whites until they form soft peaks. Fold whites into chocolate batter, 1 cup at a time. Batter will become less dense but will still be quite heavy. Spoon 1/4-inch layer of batter into bottom of each ramekin. Place a chocolate surprise in center of each ramekin. Cover surprise with remaining batter. Place ramekins in freezer. Freeze overnight.

---

continued on next page

1 cup milk
1 cup cream
1/2 vanilla bean, split or
   1 teaspoon vanilla
6 yolks
1/2 cup sugar

VANILLA CREAM SAUCE: Scald milk and cream with split vanilla bean (or 1 tablespoon vanilla). Beat yolks with sugar in mixer until light and very thick. Slowly pour hot liquid into yolk mixture, whisking constantly. Return mixture to pan and cook, stirring constantly, until thick enough to coat back of spoon. This will take 3-5 minutes. Remove from heat. Remove vanilla bean. Cool. Cover and refrigerate until ready to use. (Best if made 1 day ahead.)

Whipped cream (optional)

TO SERVE: Preheat oven to 350°F. Bake frozen chocolate ramekins on a baking sheet for 35-40 minutes. Remove from oven and let stand 4 minutes. Carefully turn each ramekin on its side and pull out soufflé. Peel parchment paper off bottom, set soufflé upright. Spoon puddle of vanilla sauce onto center of each dessert plate. Set soufflé in middle. Served with whipped cream if desired.

VARIATION: Add 1-2 tablespoons Grand Marnier to vanilla cream sauce.

Cream Cheese Crêpes
Apricot Sauce

SERVES 4-6

This is a versatile dessert for all occasions. The apricot topping can be easily changed by varying the type of jam used. I first taught this recipe in 1978 when crêpes were popular. Although crêpes are not widely served today, I suggest this recipe for that very reason. Sometimes serving an old-but-forgotten favorite is as effective as serving something trendy.

---

1 cup flour
3 eggs
2 tablespoons butter, melted
2 tablespoons sugar
1 teaspoon vanilla
Pinch of salt
1 1/2 cups milk

CRÊPES: Put flour, eggs, butter, sugar, vanilla, and salt in food processor. Process until well combined. With machine running, pour milk through feed tube. Scrape sides, if necessary. Pour finished crêpe batter into measuring cup. Lightly butter a crêpe pan. Pour in enough batter to lightly cover bottom of pan. Cook over moderately high heat until brown, about 1 minute. Turn and cook 5-10 seconds on other side. Crêpes can be stacked on top of each of each other. No need to put waxed paper in between. They can also be frozen.

Rind of 1 lemon
2 teaspoons sugar
8 ounces cream cheese, softened
1/2 stick butter, softened
2 tablespoons additional sugar
2 teaspoons vanilla

FILLING: Place rind of lemon and sugar in mini food processor. Process until rind is grated fine. Add zest to large food processor with cream cheese, butter, additional sugar, and vanilla. Process until well combined.

---

1 cup apricot jam
1/3 cup orange juice
2 tablespoons butter
Juice of 1 lemon
2 teaspoons grated lemon zest

APRICOT SAUCE: Heat apricot jam, orange juice, butter, lemon juice, and lemon zest in small saucepan until mixture is smooth and hot.

1/2 cup almonds, sliced and toasted in 250°F oven for 30 minutes

TO ASSEMBLE AND SERVE: Fill crêpes and roll up. Place in buttered ovenproof dish or individual gratin dishes. Top crêpes with sauce and sprinkle with almonds. Bake in preheated 350°F oven for 10 minutes or until crêpes are hot and sauce is bubbling.

Classic Crème Brûlée

SERVES 4-6

Here is a foolproof recipe for this popular dessert. Even though crème brûlée is served everywhere, I included it here because it is one of life's real pleasures. This version is extremely easy and light-tasting with a crunchy topping. The topping can be broiled; no special equipment is needed.

---

2 cups heavy cream
1/2 vanilla bean, split
4 egg yolks
1/4 cup granulated sugar

CUSTARD: Preheat oven to 350°F. Place cream in 2-quart saucepan. Scrape seeds out of split vanilla bean into cream. Add the split bean also. Heat cream with vanilla seeds and bean until bubbling around the edges. Do not boil. Remove bean. Beat yolks lightly, adding granulated sugar gradually. Remove cream from heat and pour into egg mixture very slowly, stirring with wooden spoon. Pour into individual 6-ounce ramekins and bake in water bath (bain marie) until set, about 45 minutes.

1/2 cup light brown sugar

TOPPING: Sprinkle tops generously with brown sugar. Place under broiler for 1-2 minutes or until sugar melts and turns dark brown. Chill for several hours or overnight.

TO SERVE: Serve cold in ramekins in which they were baked.

VARIATION: Pour 1/4-inch layer of melted chocolate on cold custard. Refrigerate. Put brown sugar on top of chocolate and broil until brown. Serve immediately or refrigerate.

NOTE: If you do not have a vanilla bean, substitute a teaspoon of good quality vanilla.

Floating Island

SERVES 6-8

I must thank Betty Moorman, my mother-in-law, for this fabulous classic. I have seen recipes for this dessert in many cookbooks, but none produces such wonderful results as this one.

1 cup milk
1 cup cream
3-inch piece of vanilla bean, split
6 egg yolks
1/2 cup sugar

CUSTARD: Combine milk and cream. Split vanilla bean and scrape seeds from bean into milk mixture. Add vanilla bean. Heat until milk is scalded. It does not need to boil. Beat yolks and sugar with an electric mixer until light colored and very thick. Pour a little of hot liquid into egg yolk mixture, stirring with whisk. Continue to combine liquid and egg yolks until well combined. Return mixture to double boiler and, while stirring constantly, continue to cook mixture until it is thick enough to coat back of spoon. It will thicken more as it cools. Remove vanilla bean, cool and refrigerate. This can be made a day before serving. (Custard will thicken much faster over direct heat. Just watch and stir it constantly to prevent eggs from curdling).

6 egg whites
1/2 cup sugar
4-6 cups skim milk

MERINGUES OR ISLANDS: Beat egg whites with an electric mixer. When peaks are close to forming, slowly begin to add sugar. Meringues are ready when stiff, but not dry, peaks form. Heat milk in 3-quart sauté pan until almost scalded. Use enough milk to have 2-inch depth of liquid in sauté pan. Do not allow milk to boil. A simmer or less is desired to cook meringues. Drop egg whites or meringues by spoonfuls into milk. Cook 2 minutes on one side and turn over. Cook 1 minute on other side. These will expand as they cook. Size of "islands" is entirely up to you. Drain on paper towels to cool. Once cool, they can be easily lifted with your hands. Place directly on cold custard.

Sliced strawberries
Shaved chocolate

TO SERVE: Place custard in wide-bottomed serving dish. Float meringues on top. "Throw" strawberries around in custard. Shave chocolate on top.

NOTE: Custard can be made several days ahead. Meringues loose some volume when made ahead, but it can be done. If possible, make "islands" the morning you will serve them.

French Lace Cookie Tacos
Mango Sauce

SERVES 8

I developed this dessert for a cooking class featuring Southwest Cuisine. As in some of my other recipes, I have taken a classic French recipe–in this case French Lace cookies–and transformed it into something new. This type of cookie is wonderful because it can be frozen and maintain its shape. Form it around small brioche molds and you have a great receptacle for multi-colored sorbets.

1/2 cup light corn syrup
1/4 cup butter
1/4 cup shortening
2/3 cup brown sugar, firmly
    packed
1 cup flour
1 cup chopped pecans

FRENCH LACE COOKIES: Preheat oven to 325°F. Combine syrup, butter, shortening, and brown sugar in saucepan. Bring mixture to boil. Once boiling, remove immediately from heat. Off heat, stir in flour and chopped nuts. Drop by rounded teaspoons onto greased cookie sheet, about 3-4 inches apart. Bake for 8-10 minutes. Cool slightly, about 30 seconds to 1 minute. When cookies are just beginning to set, fold into taco shape. (I use tops from canned goods to make my forms. Take a top you would throw away and fold it into a taco shape. Place cookie on outside of form.) Cookies can be frozen at this point.

---

2 cups heavy cream
4 tablespoons confectioners'
    sugar
Fresh fruit

FILLING: Whip cream until soft peaks begin to form. Begin adding confectioners' sugar at this time. Fill "tacos" with whipped cream and add fresh fruit.

---

1 28-ounce can mangos
    with sugar

MANGO SAUCE: Purée canned mangos in food processor. Taste. It should be perfect.

RASPBERRY SAUCE: See page 213 for recipe.

TO ASSEMBLE AND SERVE: Arrange Mango or Raspberry Sauce on a plate. Fill lace cookies with whipped cream and fresh fruit. Allow some fresh fruit to spill out. Place on top of sauces.

NOTES: When forming cookies, you must work fast. Bake no more than 6 cookies at a time. If cookies become too hard to shape, return to oven for a few seconds. When making taco forms from the lids of cans, tape sharp edges.

Strawberry Sorbet

SERVES 4

You may use this recipe as a formula for making all kinds of sorbets.
Substitute any fruit for strawberries. It's fun to make a variety of
flavors. Choose fruits or berries that are compatible in color.

---

1 cup sugar
1 cup water

SUGAR SYRUP: Put cold water in saucepan with sugar. (This recipe can be doubled or tripled.) Bring sugar-water mixture to boil. As soon as mixture boils, remove it from heat. It should be crystal clear. Cool. Refrigerate. It will keep quite a long time in refrigerator, so you might make more than you need.

---

3 pints fresh strawberries, stemmed and cut into pieces
1 tablespoon lemon juice
1 tablespoon kirsch
Sugar syrup

SORBET: Place strawberries, lemon juice, and kirsch in food processor. Process until smooth. Taste. Add sugar syrup to taste. Amount will vary each time. Freeze in an electric ice cream maker until frozen. Shape into balls with a small ice cream scoop. Freeze them in plastic bags. (They will stay nice this way for 1-2 days.)

TO SERVE: Make French Lace Cookie basket by forming warm French Lace Cookies around a small 2-inch tart mold. See page 208 for recipe. Fill with balls of sorbet.

VARIATION: Serve with Raspberry or Mango Sauce.

Lemon Curd Base
Lemon Curd Dessert Sauce

MAKES 2 CUPS

This recipe for lemon curd is the basis for a variety of desserts. It is a wonderful recipe to have on hand as you can turn it into many different spectacular and tasty desserts.

6 egg yolks
Pinch of salt
1 cup sugar
1/2 cup fresh lemon juice
1 teaspoon lemon rind, grated

LEMON CURD BASE: Place yolks, salt, sugar, lemon juice, and rind in top of double boiler. Cook over hot water, stirring constantly, until mixture thickens and coats back of spoon. Remove from heat. Cool. Cover with plastic wrap. Will keep in refrigerator 1 week.

Lemon curd base
Water

LEMON CURD DESSERT SAUCE: Use only as much of the lemon curd base as is necessary. Add water by tablespoons, stirring constantly to reach desired sauce consistency. There are commercial brands on the market, but the one you make at home is infinitely better.

NOTE: *Lemon Curd will thicken faster if you cook it directly over the heat rather than in a double boiler. The use of a double boiler is for security, to be sure it does not heat too fast and curdle the egg yolks.*

Cornucopias with Lemon Cream Raspberry Sauce

SERVES 6-8

This idea was inspired by Roger Vergé, a noted French chef. I have simplified it somewhat. It is a beautiful dessert to serve in the fall. Cornucopias can be made ahead and frozen. Lemon Curd can be made up to one week ahead and Raspberry Sauce can be made a week ahead or longer if frozen. Because all can be done ahead, it is an easy dish to turn out the day of a party.

---

1 box frozen puff pastry, defrosted in refrigerator
Cornet molds, 2x2 1/2-inch or cream horn molds
Egg glaze, (1 egg beaten with 1 tablespoon water)

CORNUCOPIAS: Preheat oven to 400°F. On lightly floured work surface or pastry cloth, roll out one sheet of pastry as thin as possible. Cut into 1/2-inch strips down length of sheet. Beginning at pointed end of cornet molds, wrap one band of pastry around each mold, overlapping strip as you work around in spiral pattern. Cut off any excess pastry. Paint finished cornet molds with egg glaze. This will serve as glue to hold cornucopias together and also serve as a browning agent. Place on baking sheet and bake for 15-20 minutes or until brown.

Lemon curd
2 cups heavy cream, whipped

FILLING: Make Lemon Curd (see recipe on page 212.) Whip cream and fold into cold lemon curd.

---

2 12-ounce sacks frozen raspberries
2-3 tablespoons raspberry jelly
Juice of 1 lemon
Sugar to taste, about 1/2-1 cup

RASPBERRY SAUCE: Defrost berries. Put into food processor with jelly and lemon juice. Purée. Place purée into a saucepan and heat with the sugar until the sugar and jelly are melted. Remove from the heat and strain. Refrigerate until ready to serve.

Fresh berries

TO ASSEMBLE AND SERVE: Place Raspberry Sauce on bottom of individual plates. Fill cornucopia with lemon cream mixture and place on plates. Allow some lemon cream to spill out onto plate. Arrange variety of fresh fruit onto lemon cream. (I have found berries of different types look and taste the best.)

Lemon Custard Tart

SERVES 6-8

This tart was once the specialty at Freddy Girardet's restaurant in Switzerland. I revised a recipe published in Pleasure of Cooking *many years ago. The original recipe states that you cannot prepare the tart ahead, but I tried it and it works fine.*

---

1 1/4 cups flour
Pinch of salt
8 tablespoons butter,
   cut into 8 pieces
1/3 cup cold water

Or, use Pillsbury ready-made
   pie crust

PASTRY: Place flour and salt in food processor. Process once. Add butter and mix it into flour using on-off turns until mixture resembles "little peas." With machine running, pour in water. Stop machine immediately before pastry forms a ball. Form final ball with hands. Dough should be right temperature to work immediately. Fit dough into regular 9-inch glass pie plate. Prick bottom with fork. Refrigerate until ready to use.

---

4 large eggs
1 1/2 cups sugar
Zest of 1/2 orange, grated
1/2 cup fresh lemon juice
1/2 cup fresh orange juice
1/4 cup heavy cream

FILLING: Preheat oven to 400°F. Put eggs, sugar, orange zest, lemon juice, orange juice, and cream in processor and process for about 1 minute or until smooth. Pour filling into unbaked pie shell and bake for 25-35 minutes. When filling is browned and moves only slightly, remove from oven. Allow to cool. Filling will firm up as it cools. Refrigerate several hours or overnight.

Confectioners' sugar

TO SERVE: Sprinkle with confectioners' sugar before serving.

NOTE: This is prettiest served in a 10-inch quiche pan, at least 1 1/2 inches deep. You will need to double the filling. No need to double the pastry recipe.

Frozen Lemon Tower with Fresh Fruit

SERVES 12-14

In creating this recipe, I simply adapted a wonderful old recipe for Lemon Bavarian by molding it into ring molds of different sizes. When stacked, they form a tower. In the original recipe, it was frozen in a glass dish with graham cracker crumbs as the bottom layer. I use this recipe to illustrate that tried-and-true dishes are often the building blocks of new cuisine.

1/3 box graham crackers
1/2 cup brown sugar
1/2 cup pecans
1 stick butter, melted
2 bottomless ring molds
  (10-inch and 7-inch)

CRUST: Place graham crackers, brown sugar, and pecans in food processor. Process until crackers and pecans are minced. With machine running, pour melted butter through feed tube. Cover an unrimmed baking sheet with plastic wrap. Place two ring molds, one smaller than other, on baking sheets. Divide crust between two ring molds, pressing it firmly in bottom. Refrigerate.

---

6 egg yolks
Pinch of salt
1 cup sugar
1/2 cup fresh lemon juice
1 teaspoon lemon rind, grated
2 cups heavy cream, whipped

FILLING: Place yolks, salt, sugar, lemon juice, and rind in top of double boiler. Cook over hot water, stirring constantly until mixture thickens and coats back of spoon. Remove from heat. Cool. Beat cream until stiff. Fold into cooled lemon mixture. Pour into two ring molds. Freeze.

---

1 cup heavy cream
2 tablespoons confectioners'
  sugar
Fresh fruit such as grapes,
  berries, sliced peaches,
  sliced apples, etc.

TO ASSEMBLE: Remove rings from freezer. Allow to sit for several minutes. Run knife around outside of molds. Rings will come loose easily. Place larger lemon mold on large flat platter. Place small lemon mold on top of larger one. Whip heavy cream until stiff peaks begin to form. Add sugar. Continue to whip until cream is stiff enough to use as an icing. Ice "tower" with whipped cream. Decorate top and sides with fresh fruit.

TO SERVE: Slice and give each guest a piece accompanied by some fresh fruit. You could also serve it with Lemon Curd or Raspberry Sauces. See pages 212 and 213.

NOTE: *In photograph on page 130, I used three ring molds of different sizes for a more glamorous effect.*

Tiny Tarts with Lemon Curd

SERVES 8-10

*This is a recipe we do often for large buffets. I make the shells in a
variety of shapes and then arrange them on trays close to the coffee.
These are light, refreshing and easy.*

Pillsbury Pie Crust

TART SHELLS: Preheat oven to 400°F. Cut dough into
shapes to fit small tart shells. Press another mold exactly
like it on top. Bake for 15-20 minutes or until done. Allow
to cool.

---

6 egg yolks
Pinch of salt
1 cup sugar
1/2 cup fresh lemon juice
1 teaspoon lemon rind, grated
1/2-3/4 cup heavy cream,
  not whipped

LEMON CURD: Place yolks, salt, sugar, lemon juice, and rind
in top of double boiler. Cook over hot water, stirring
constantly, until mixture thickens and coats back of spoon.
Remove from heat. Cool. Reserve until ready to use. Before
filling tarts, stir in cream to thin down lemon curd. Fill
tart shells and freeze.

---

1 cup heavy cream
2 tablespoons confectioners'
  sugar

TO ASSEMBLE: Remove tarts from freezer. Whip heavy
cream. When peaks begin to form, whip in confectioners'
sugar. Put into pastry bag fitted with a star tip and pipe
cream on top of tiny tarts. I try to make a variety of
designs—one simple rosette, lines of cream, x's, dots in
corners, or anything that comes to mind. You may also
embellish them with candied violets.

TO SERVE: Arrange on trays for large buffet or place two
to three on individual dessert plates.

NOTE: *Begin to collect different shapes of small tart shells.
Whenever I buy a different shape, I buy two. Then I can
place raw pastry dough in one and press the other shape on
top. This keeps shell from rising up when baked. The top is
removed after baking.*

Fresh Lime Pie

MAKES 1 PIE

My mother-in-law introduced me to this recipe when I was first married. It is an especially refreshing summer dessert and always a great hit with men.

3/4 stick butter, melted
1/3 cup light brown sugar
2 cups graham cracker crumbs

CRUST: Melt butter with brown sugar. Crush graham crackers in food processor or buy box of crushed graham crackers. Add graham cracker crumbs to butter-sugar mixture. Stir well until crumbs are moist. Press graham crackers firmly into bottom and sides of 9-inch pie plate. Refrigerate.

1/3 cup cornstarch
1/2 teaspoon salt
1/4 cup cold water
1/2 cup sugar
1 1/4 cups boiling water
2 tablespoons butter
Peel of 1 lime
1/2 cup sugar
3 egg yolks
1/3 cup fresh lime juice
1 teaspoon vanilla

FILLING: Combine cornstarch, salt, cold water, and sugar in top of double boiler. Mix well. Gradually add hot water. Cook 3-5 minutes over rapidly boiling water until thick, stirring constantly with a wire whisk. Cover. Let sit 2-3 minutes until thick. Add butter. Place lime peel and 1/2 cup sugar in mini food processor. Process to create zest. Lightly beat egg yolks with sugar and zest. Add lime juice. Add a little hot cornstarch mixture. Slowly begin to add remaining cornstarch mixture. Return to double boiler. Cook, uncovered, stirring with a wooden spoon, for 5 minutes or until very thick. Remove from heat. Add vanilla. Pour into prepared pie shell. Cover with plastic wrap. Refrigerate until very cold, several hours or overnight.

1 cup heavy cream
2 tablespoons confectioners' sugar

TOPPING: Whip cream until stiff peaks begin to form. Add confectioners' sugar and continue to whip cream until it is stiff.

TO ASSEMBLE AND SERVE: Remove plastic wrap and top with whipped cream. If desired, decorate with thin slices of lime.

Macadamia Nut Pie

SERVES 6-8

*I first tasted Macadamia Nut Pie at Arcadia Restaurant in New York.
Not privy to their recipe, I spent years perfecting my own version of
this delicious dessert. Here is my attempt at this special treat.*

Pillsbury pastry shell

PASTRY SHELL: Preheat oven to 400°F. Place Pillsbury pastry into one pie shell or 6 individual shells. Refrigerate until cold and firm. Prick bottom and fill shell with pie weights, dried beans or another pie shell. Bake shells with weights for 10 minutes. Remove weights and continue to bake an additional 10 minutes or until shell is golden.

1/2 pound macadamia nuts,
   or 2 4 1/2-ounce cans
1 cup sugar
1/4 cup water
1 cup heavy cream

FILLING: Toast nuts in 350°F oven for 5-7 minutes. Watch carefully, as they burn easily. Turn several times. Chop coarsely. Melt sugar with water in 2-quart saucepan over low heat until mixture is perfectly clear. Turn heat to high and cook mixture until it begins to turn a caramel color. Twirl saucepan by handle; do not use spoon. When mixture is a nice caramel color, add cream and stir constantly until smooth. Mixture will spatter and tighten up a little before smoothing out. Add nuts. Return mixture to boil. Boil for 2 minutes. Pour into prebaked pie shell. Refrigerate until cold and firm.

1 cup grated coconut
1 1/2 cups heavy cream
3 tablespoons confectioners'
   sugar

TOPPING: Toast coconut in slow 250°-300°F oven until lightly browned, about 10 minutes. Stir once or twice. Whip cream until soft peaks form. Add sugar by tablespoons and continue to whip cream until firm peaks form.

TO ASSEMBLE: Spread whipped cream on top of pie and sprinkle with toasted coconut.

VARIATION: Use one half macadamia nuts and one half walnuts.

Adelaide's Peach Cobbler

SERVES 6-8

Adelaide Thompson, one of the best country cooks I know, gave me
this recipe. Since Adelaide does not measure or really follow recipes,
I had her make this cobbler in front of me. I wrote instructions as
she worked. It is a treasured recipe I never want to lose.

---

2 28-ounce cans peaches,
  drained
2 2/3 cups sugar
1 1/2 teaspoons flour
1/2 teaspoon cinnamon
1 teaspoon nutmeg
1 stick butter, melted
1 teaspoon vanilla
1/4 cup cream (optional)

PEACH FILLING: Mash peaches with potato masher. You do not want a purée. Place in saucepan with sugar, flour, cinnamon, and nutmeg. Cook over moderately high heat until thick and bubbling. Brown butter over moderately high heat in separate saucepan. Watch carefully so it browns but does not burn. Add browned butter to spiced peaches. Cook 10-15 minutes or until bubbling again. Remove from heat. Add vanilla and heavy cream. Stir and set aside to cool.

---

3 cups flour
1/4 teaspoon baking powder
1/2 teaspoon sugar
1/2 teaspoon salt
16 tablespoons Crisco
1/2-3/4 cup ice cold water
Sugar (optional)
Nutmeg (optional)

TEXAS COUNTRY PASTRY: Place flour, baking powder, sugar, salt, and Crisco in food processor. Process until crumbly. Add 1/2 cup ice cold water and process just until a ball starts to form. Form dough into a ball with your hands. Refrig-erate for 30 minutes if dough is too soft. Roll out half the dough. Place in 2-quart oven proof 13x9x2-inch baking dish. (Do not use glass.) Prick bottom with fork. Place peach mixture over unbaked crust. Roll out other half of dough. Place on top of peaches, pinching edges to seal. Prick top in several places with fork. Sprinkle top with additional sugar and nutmeg if desired. Refrigerate until ready to bake.

1/2 stick butter
1 teaspoon nutmeg
1/3-1/2 cup sugar

TOPPING: Preheat oven to 375°F. Melt butter and combine with nutmeg and sugar. Pour over top of cobbler and bake for 45 minutes.

Vanilla ice cream (optional)
Whipped cream (optional)

TO SERVE: Cut into squares to serve. Serve with vanilla ice cream or a dollop of sweetened whipped cream.

NOTE: Adelaide says to add 1 teaspoon vinegar and 1 egg to the water if you are a beginning pastry chef. It makes the dough easy to roll out.

Pear Tart

SERVES 6-8

This was requested by so many of my students, I had to include it.
Personally, I did not know it was so widely used and appreciated.
This dessert is incredibly easy, especially if you use a Pillsbury
ready-made pie crust instead of making your own.

---

1 3/4 cups flour
10 tablespoons unsalted
   butter
1/4 cup sugar
2 egg yolks
1/4 cup water
1 teaspoon vanilla

Or, use Pillsbury ready-made
   pie crust

PASTRY: Combine flour, butter, and sugar in food processor. Mix using on-off pulses. Do this until butter resembles "little peas." This should take no more than 5-8 pulses. With machine running, add egg yolks and liquids through feed tube. Process until dough almost forms ball. Remove from processor and form into ball with your hands. Dough can be used immediately. Roll out and place in 9-inch pie plate or 10-inch quiche pan.

---

1 1/4 cups sugar
6 tablespoons flour
3 eggs
1 1/2 sticks butter, melted and
   cooled
2-4 pears, peeled and cored

FILLING: Combine sugar, flour, and eggs in bowl of food processor. Process until smooth. Melt butter over moderately high heat until golden brown. Cool. Once cool, turn on food processor with egg mixture and slowly pour in butter through feed tube. Quarter pears and cut each quarter into 8 thin slices. Keeping one side intact, fan out slices.

TO ASSEMBLE: Preheat oven to 350°F. Arrange pears opposite each other in unbaked pastry shell. You may need 3-4 pears if they are small. Be sure pear slices fan out slightly. Pour batter around pears, leaving backs of pears uncovered by liquid. Bake until filling is firm and nicely browned, about 1 hour.

TO SERVE: Serve warm or at room temperature. Very good with ice cream. I would bring an entire pie to the table and then serve it. It is very pretty and should be seen. If you are serving buffet style, have one whole pie for display and another pie cut into slices.

Kathryn's Pecan Pie

SERVES 8

This is a foolproof and fabulous recipe that came from my sister, Kathryn.

1 1/4 cups flour
Pinch of salt
1 stick butter, cut into 8
    tablespoons
1/3 cup cold water

Or, use Pillsbury ready-made
    pie crust

STANDARD CRUST: Put flour and salt in food processor. Quickly process once. Add butter. Process with on-off motions until butter is size of "little peas." Once this has happened, turn machine on and pour water through feed tube. When dough is about to form ball, remove it from machine and form it into ball with your hands. This dough will be ready to use immediately. Roll out dough and place in 9-inch pie shell. Prick bottom and refrigerate until ready to use.

1/2 cup white sugar
1 cup brown sugar
2 tablespoons flour
2 eggs
2 tablespoons milk
1 teaspoon vanilla
1/2 cup melted butter
1-2 cups pecan halves

TO PREPARE PIE: Preheat oven to 375°F. Combine white and brown sugar and flour in mixing bowl. Add eggs, milk, vanilla, butter, and pecan halves. Pour into unbaked pie shell. Bake 50 minutes or until set. Let cool. Refrigerate if not serving immediately.

TO SERVE: Reheat, if desired, for 10-15 minutes in 350°F oven. Serve hot, room temperature, or cold. Great with ice cream.

NOTE: Double filling if using a deep dish 10-inch quiche pan.

221

Strawberry Ice "Peppers" Mango Sauce

SERVES 8-10

This recipe is a variation of an old favorite. Originally, the strawberry purée was frozen in a ring mold. Once unmolded, the center was filled with sweetened whipped cream and fresh, whole strawberries. This is still a beautiful choice. However, cutting the ice with cookie cutters into unique shapes is also versatile and fun. For this recipe I found a cutter in the shape of a pepper. The mango sauce is incredibly easy and the contrasting colors look spectacular.

---

3 12-ounce bags strawberries, frozen, no sugar added
Sugar to taste
Juice of 2 lemons
3 cups water

ICE: Put berries, sugar, lemon juice, and water in blender. Blend into smooth purée. Taste for sweetness. Place puréed mixture in baking dish that can go into freezer. (You will need a baking dish that will allow 1-inch thick frozen ice.) Freeze until solid. Use cookie cutter to cut into desired shapes. (You must let ice sit out several minutes to make cutting possible.) Refreeze shaped ice in plastic bags until ready to use.

---

1 28-ounce can mangos, undrained

MANGO SAUCE: Purée canned mangos in food processor or blender.

TO SERVE: Place Mango Sauce on dessert or dinner plate. Top with Strawberry Ice Peppers.

NOTE: *When I serve desserts individually, I like to use large dinner plates instead of dessert plates.*

Index